MONTEREY'S COOKIN'

Pisto Style

FROM SICILY TO MONTEREY

By John Pisto

INTRODUCTION
William Rice,
Food & Wine Columnist, *Chicago Tribune*

ILLUSTRATIONS
Virginia Medina

HISTORICAL PHOTOGRAPHS
The Pat Hathaway Collection

CONCEPT, DESIGN, EDITOR
Riddell & Riddell
P.O. Box 51201, Pacific Grove, CA 93950

PUBLISHER
Pisto's Kitchen
763 Wave Street, Monterey, CA 93940

Monterey's Cookin' Pisto Style:
From Sicily to Monterey

ISBN 0-9640828-0-2

Pisto's Kitchen
763 Wave Street, Monterey, California 93940
PRINTED IN THE USA

This cookbook is dedicated
to my parents,
Santo and Santa Pisto,
whose love and encouragement is
the foundation of my success.

Manuel Balestreri

**HISTORIC FISHERMAN'S WHARF,
MONTEREY, CALIFORNIA**

TABLE OF CONTENTS

❖

Introduction

By William Rice

My first meeting with John Pisto is an echo, I'm sure, of hundreds of encounters others have had with him over the years. It was 1976, the year of our nation's bicentennial. I'd come anonymously to the Whaling Station, a restaurant chosen at random from a guide book, and had been charmed by the decor, put at ease by the service and thrilled to be served such local treats as artichokes from Castroville, fish caught in Monterey Bay and wines made in Monterey County.

I asked to meet the owner. In time a big bear of a man appeared, and he immediately asked, "What can I do for you?" He soon had me entranced with his enthusiasm for local products and his (at that time) avant garde theory that they should be cooked and served in the most pristine way possible. Even though I had already eaten, he felt it was necessary to cook "a few things" to illustrate what he was telling me and, as night follows day, there had to be wine to accompany the food. Once it

William Rice—Food & Wine Columnist, *Chicago Tribune*

was established I was a food journalist, he began asking questions—at least two to each query of mine—about restaurant cooking, menus and wine lists elsewhere.

When I returned to my newspaper, the *Washington Post* at that time, I wrote a story citing the Whaling Station and Ray's Boat House in Seattle as harbingers of an era when American-born and trained chefs would proudly produce original dishes featuring seasonal ingredients from their indigenous locale or region.

WILLIAM RICE—CONTINUED

I'd stumbled onto what became known as the "New American Cuisine Movement," and John Pisto became one of its founding fathers.

Since then I've accompanied John to farms and wineries and on fishing expeditions out on his beloved bay and beyond. Wherever he goes, John carries with him an aura of energy and enthusiasm, and endless curiosity. More to the point here, he brings these same qualities into his kitchen.

Too many people who teach cooking and/or write cookbooks these days talk simple, talk healthy, then go ahead and produce the same dishes they have for years—elaborately complex, fat-saturated recipes that suit neither our digestion nor our style of living.

As anyone who has watched him cook on television knows, John Pisto is different. Simple, quick cooking is second nature to him. Healthy ingredients are virtually the only ones he knew growing up on what recently has become famous as "the Mediterranean diet."

As an adult cook and host, he gives new dimensions to the Italian term *abbondanza.*

Like John himself, this book is direct and uncompromising. A cookbook without desserts? John doesn't do desserts and he won't pretend he does. But should someone have dared suggest he eliminate garlic to win over fastidious cooks, he would have laughed and refused to.

Journalists are supposed to reduce complex issues to simple terms. So, in searching for a single word that would sum up John, I suddenly realized that "gusto" does it. Had "gusto" not existed, someone would have coined it to sum up his approach to life and cooking. The secret ingredient that makes his food great is people. When you prepare these recipes, gather family, friends and even new acquaintances to talk and taste, to sip and laugh.

This book is John's gift to Americans of all ethnic origins. Along with its recipes, it tells an only-in-America success story that's worth sharing in these troubled times.

Craig Riddell 4

JOHN PISTO, AT HOME IN HIS KITCHEN

California
Italian Cuisine

John Pisto is a first generation Californian from an old Sicilian family. His unique style of cooking combines traditional Italian recipes and techniques with California's bounty of fresh seafood, fruits and vegetables. The result is mouth-watering dishes that are simple to prepare.

Within these pages, John shares a view of Monterey's Italian heritage and his own experiences growing up in an Italian family in Monterey, California. His lighthearted story will provide some insight as to how these recipes evolved.

Before you prepare the enclosed recipes I invite you to read page 99, titled Cooking with John Pisto.

Shopping List:

A number of staples are used in John Pisto's recipes, and these ingredients should be on hand when using this cookbook:

- Braids of fresh garlic
- Vine ripe tomatoes or canned Italian tomatoes
- Fresh Italian flat-leaf parsley
- Fresh basil
- Olive oil (John prefers unrefined, extra virgin)

SOME OF THE FIRST IMMIGRATING ITALIANS IN THEIR FELUCCAS, CIRCA 1900.

The Italians began to immigrate to Monterey in great numbers during the early 1900s. They brought with them considerable fishing skills attributed to the experience of generations fishing the Mediterranean. At the time, there were several small fleets fishing for salmon and tiny silver fish called sardines.

This fairly large exodus from Italy and Sicily is attributed to one Sicilian fisherman by the name of Pietro "Pete" Ferrante. Pete came to Monterey in 1904 and quickly gained a reputation as a man of vision and considerable fishing talent. It was Pete who designed a variation of the Italian lampara net that would change Monterey's fishing industry forever.

SEAFOOD

Barbecued Sardines • Stuffed Sardines • Poached
Monterey Halibut • Grilled Sandabs • Grilled
Mahi-Mahi • Blackened Salmon • Salmon with
Pasta & Marinara • Swordfish with Garlic &
Lemon Paste • Swordfish with Caramelized
Onions • Swordfish Mediterranean Style •
Swordfish with Italian Salsa • Pasta Capri •
Bouillabaisse California Style • Lazy Man's
Cioppino • Pisto's Scampi • Sicilian Marinated
Crab • Sicilian Crab Pasta • Spicy Clams &
Mussels with Pasta • Rock Fish Chowder • Rock
Fish in Coconut Milk • Rock Fish Cancun Style •
Rock Fish French Style • Rock Fish in Parchment
• Rock Fish with Pasta

BARBEQUED SARDINES

SERVES 2

- 6 lg. Monterey sardines
- 4 tblsp. cracked peppercorns
- ½ cup rock salt
- 3 tblsp. ground cumin or Pisto's Moroccan Spice

Scale and gut fish, leaving on head and tail. Coat fish with rock salt and roll in cumin and fresh cracked pepper. Set aside for approximately 1 hour.

Prepare barbecue grill or cast iron stovetop grill. Place sardines on hot grill. Cook for approximately 3-5 minutes on each side or until done.

STUFFED SARDINES

SERVES 1-2

- 6 large Monterey sardines
- 1½ cups seasoned bread crumbs
- ¼ cup raisins
- 2 tblsp. pine nuts
- ¼ cup Parmesan cheese
- olive oil
- ¼ cup white wine
- 1 lemon
- salt & black pepper to taste

Cut off sardine heads, gut and scale. Remove backbone by running thumb up and down spine. Butterfly sardines.

Mix bread crumbs with raisins, pine nuts, cheese, salt and pepper. Brush olive oil on sardines. Fill sardine cavity with bread crumb mixture.

Pre-heat oven to 350⁰. Roll sardines from head to tail and place in baking dish. Sprinkle with wine, oil and additional bread crumb mixture. Bake for 20-30 minutes or until well done. Serve with lemon garnish.

THE *GERALDINE-ANN* WITH AN EXCEPTIONALLY LARGE CATCH OF SARDINES.

Shortly after his new net was put to use, Pete summoned his Italian friends and relatives to Monterey and they, in turn, encouraged others to embark on an adventure to the new land. Among those daring fishermen were men with family names as rich as Balesteri, Cutino, Russo, Verga, Alliotti and Cardinelli—names that are still very much a part of Monterey today.

It was with their arrival that Monterey began to blossom into a major fishing port, soon to become the "Sardine Capitol of the World."

POACHED MONTEREY HALIBUT

SERVES 4

- *4 8-10 oz. fillets of halibut*
- *1 bunch Italian flat-leaf parsley*
- *6 garlic cloves*
- *1 ripe tomato*
- *3 lemons*
- *olive oil*
- *3 cups water*
- *1 cup white wine*
- *salt & black pepper to taste*

Chop parsley and garlic coarsely. Dice tomato. Extract the juice from 2 lemons. Place oil, water, wine, and lemon juice in a cast iron skillet over medium-high heat. Stir in garlic, parsley and tomato. Cook for approximately 10 minutes. Add fish to skillet. Season with salt and pepper. Cover skillet and poach fish for approximately 8-10 minutes (test with a fork for white flaky fillets)—do not overcook! When fish is done, remove fillets from skillet and reduce remaining liquid to about 2 cups.

Serve fish on platter with sauce and garnish with lemon slices.

IN THEIR HEYDAY, THE ITALIAN FISHERMEN HAULED IN MORE THAN 200,000 TONS OF SARDINES EACH SEASON.

GRILLED SANDABS

SERVES 2

- 2 8-oz. fillets
- 1 cup flour
- olive oil
- 1 lb. baby greens
- salt & black pepper to taste
- lemon wedges

Season fillets with salt and pepper, then coat generously with flour. Cover the bottom of a non-stick skillet with olive oil and pre-heat over a medium-high flame until hot. Carefully place fish in skillet and cook for 3-4 minutes on each side, turning only once. Remove fish from skillet and place on towels to remove excess oil.

Serve on a bed of baby greens with lemon garnish.

GRILLED MAHI-MAHI

SERVES 4

- 4 ½"-thick mahi-mahi steaks
- 4 garlic cloves
- ¼ bunch fresh Italian flat-leaf parsley
- ¼ bunch fresh oregano
- olive oil
- 1 tsp. water
- 1 lemon (juice only)
- 2 tblsp. Pisto's Sensational Seasoning
- salt & black pepper

To prepare sauce, chop garlic, parsley and oregano coarsely. Cover the bottom of a large skillet with olive oil. Place over high heat. Add garlic, parsley, oregano and salt and pepper. Cook for 3 minutes. Add 1 teaspoon water and the juice of 1 lemon. Bring to a boil, then remove from heat.

Pre-heat your stovetop grill for 10 minutes or until smoking. Brush fish with olive oil and coat both sides with Sensational Seasoning. Grill fish for 3-5 minutes on both sides or until done. Place on serving platter and baste with sauce. Serve hot.

MONTEREY'S RUGGED YET PRISTINE COASTLINE HAS BEEN COMPARED TO THE SHORES OF SICILY, CIRCA 1880.   PHOTO BY JOHNSON

Although my father was not a fisherman (he was a tailor by trade), the lure of friends, family and the often talked about Mediterranean climate found in Monterey grew all too tempting.

We arrived in Monterey in 1941, just before the war and in the last few years of the Steinbeck era. We immediately felt at home with the rugged coastline, the neighborhood Italian grocers, and the bocce ball games by the waterfront.

BLACKENED SALMON

- *6 cleaned and boned 8-oz. salmon steaks*
- *½ cup Pisto's Sensational Seasoning*
- *¼ cup butter*

Pour Sensational Seasoning into pie pan. Melt butter in large pan over low heat. Pour into a separate pie pan. Prepare stovetop grill or skillet by heating until smoking hot.

Dip fish into butter (or butter may be applied with a brush), then into seasoning, covering salmon on both sides. Shake off excess seasoning. Place fish into skillet and grill for 5-7 minutes on each side, or longer, depending on the size of the fillet.

Using a fan is recommended to avoid breathing in fumes. These fumes can cause irritation to the eyes and lungs.

(This method is not recommended for thick cuts.)

SALMON WITH PASTA & MARINARA

SERVES 2-4

- *2 cleaned and boned 8-oz. salmon steaks*
- *Marinara sauce (recipe pg. 66)*
- *2 tblsp. capers*
- *¼ cup pitted Calamata olives*
- *½ lb. penné pasta*
- *salt & black pepper to taste*

Cut salmon into 1-inch cubes. Prepare Italian marinara sauce. Add capers, olives and salmon to sauce. Cook sauce over medium heat for approximately 30 minutes, stirring as necessary to prevent scorching.

Prepare pasta in salted, boiling water. Drain pasta.

Place pasta in a large serving bowl, cover with sauce. Mix well and serve.

SALMON CAUGHT IN MONTEREY BAY, CAL.

FAR MORE THAN SARDINES FLOURISHED IN MONTEREY BAY, AS SHOWN IN THIS EARLY POSTCARD.

Although sardines were the primary catch, Monterey Bay was also loaded with salmon, rock fish, mackerel and many other varieties.

These fish were virtually ignored throughout the sardine boom, leaving them to flourish for almost three decades.

SWORDFISH WITH GARLIC & LEMON PASTE

SERVES 2

- 2 1"-thick swordfish steaks
- ½ lemon
- 1 tomato
- ¼ bunch Italian flat-leaf parsley
- 6 garlic cloves
- 3 tsp. rock salt
- olive oil
- 4 tblsp. Pisto's Sensational Seasoning

To make garlic sauce you will need a mortar and pestle. Squeeze juice from lemon then dice lemon rind. Remove juice and seeds from tomato and dice it. Chop parsley coarsely.

Place garlic cloves and rock salt in mortar. Crush into a paste while drizzling a teaspoon of olive oil into mixture as a binding agent. Add diced tomato, parsley and lemon rind. Grind mixture into a firm paste.

Pre-heat your stovetop grill for 10 minutes or until smoking. Paint swordfish with olive oil on both sides. Then cover both sides with Sensational Seasoning. Place fish on grill and cook for 5 minutes on each side, or until done. Test for solid white meat with a fork. Do not serve rare. Remove swordfish from grill and paint with lemon paste. Serve immediately.

SWORDFISH WITH CARAMELIZED ONIONS

SERVES 2

- 2 1"-thick swordfish steaks
- 1 cup white wine
- ½ cup raisins
- 2 med. yellow onions
- 1 tsp. sugar
- ¼ cup capers
- ¼ cup pine nuts
- 5 tsp. red wine vinegar
- 1 lemon
- sprig of parsley
- 3 tblsp. Sensational Seasoning

Soak raisins in white wine until plump. To caramelize onions, cut off root area and peel away the first layer of skin. Cut into thin rings. Prepare a small frying pan with olive oil. Place onions in pan and sauté. Stir in sugar. When onions begin to soften, add raisins, capers, pine nuts and vinegar. Stir until onions begin to brown. Remove from heat.

Pre-heat your stovetop grill for 10 minutes or until smoking. Paint swordfish with olive oil on both sides. Then cover both sides with Sensational Seasoning. Place fish on grill and cook for 5-7 minutes on both sides, or until done. Test for solid white meat with a fork. Do not serve rare.

Pour onion mixture on a serving platter and place swordfish over bed of onions. Garnish with parsley and lemon and serve.

Swordfish Mediterranean Style

SERVES 4

- 4 1"-thick swordfish steaks
- 4 garlic cloves
- ¼ bunch fresh basil
- ½ cup capers

- olive oil
- 1 lemon (juice only)
- 3 tblsp. Pisto's Sensational Seasoning
- salt & black pepper to taste

To prepare Mediterranean sauce you will need a small frying pan. Chop garlic, basil and capers coarsely. Sauté garlic in frying pan with olive oil. Add basil, salt and pepper. Add capers and stir until garlic is soft. Remove from heat and add the juice from the lemon. Set aside.

Pre-heat your stovetop grill for 10 minutes or until smoking. Paint swordfish with olive oil on both sides. Then coat fish with Sensational Seasoning. Place fish on grill and cook for 5-7 minutes on both sides, or until done. Test for solid white meat with a fork. Do not serve rare. Spoon sauce over swordfish and serve.

Swordfish with Italian Salsa

SERVES 4

- 4 ½"-thick swordfish steaks
- 6 garlic cloves
- ¼ bunch fresh basil
- 2 ripe tomatoes
- olive oil
- ¼ bunch fresh basil

- 2 tblsp. pitted green olives
- ¼ cup capers
- 3 tsp. balsamic vinegar
- 3 tblsp. Pisto's Sensational Seasoning
- salt & black pepper to taste

To prepare Italian salsa you will need a small frying pan. Chop garlic and basil coarsely. Cut out stem area of tomatoes and squeeze out excess juice. Peel and chop into pulp.

Sauté garlic in olive oil. Add basil, salt, pepper, olives and capers. When garlic starts to soften add tomato pulp and balsamic vinegar. Sauté for 5 minutes.

Pre-heat your stovetop grill for 10 minutes or until smoking. Paint swordfish with olive oil on both sides. Then coat fish with Sensational Seasoning. Place fish on grill and cook for 5-7 minutes on both sides, or until done. Test for solid white meat with a fork. Do not serve rare. Spoon salsa over swordfish and serve.

Pasta Capri—A Domenico's Original

PERHAPS THE MOST COPIED DISH IN MONTEREY!

SERVES 2

- ½ lb. linguini pasta
- olive oil
- 6 oz. butter
- ½ cup sliced black olives
- 2 med. shallots
- 6 green onions
- lemon & parsley garnish

- 1 ripe tomato
- 2 tblsp. green olives
- 1 ripe tomato
- 12 oz. bay shrimp, cooked and peeled
- ¼ cup white wine
- fresh cracked black pepper

Cook pasta in lightly salted, boiling water. Drain and toss lightly with 1 oz. olive oil. Chop onions and shallots coarsely. Dice tomato. Slice olives. Pre-heat a large, oiled sauté pan over high heat. Add butter, shrimp, tomatoes, onions and sauté for 1 minute. Add shallots, olives and black pepper and sauté for 1 minute. Add wine, reduce heat and simmer until creamy. Add more wine or pasta water if it becomes too dry. Place drained pasta in bowl and pour mixture on top of pasta. Garnish with sliced lemon and parsley.

Bouillabaisse California Style

SERVES 4-6

- 1 lb. each: fresh rock cod, halibut, swordfish, mahi-mahi, sea scallops, clams, mussels; cleaned and boned as necessary
- 1 large dungeness crab, cracked and portioned
- 1 lobster tail (cut into pieces)
- 8 large prawns, cleaned
- 6 oz. calamari, cleaned
- 4 garlic cloves, minced

- 1 tsp. fresh fennel, finely chopped
- ½ cup onions, chopped
- ½ cup leeks, chopped
- 2 bay leaves, crushed
- pinch of saffron
- olive oil
- 8 cups fish stock
- salt & black pepper

In a large frying pan, sauté garlic, fennel, onion, leeks, saffron, bay leaves, salt and pepper in olive oil until vegetables are transparent. Set aside. Cut all fish into 1-inch cubes and scrub all shellfish. Place seafood, fish stock and vegetable mixture in a 6-quart saucepan. Cook on high heat for 20-25 minutes or until clams open. Serve bouillabaisse with fresh, crusty Italian bread.

WHEN NOT AT SEA, THE FISHERMEN WOULD SPEND THEIR TIME REPAIRING AND MAINTAINING THE BOATS AND THE HUGE PURSE-SEINES USED FOR CATCHING SARDINES.

PHOTO BY SEIDENCK

My father continued to make a good living as a tailor, while I spent much of my time down at the wharf with the Italian fishermen.

Soon, the excitement of the catch was in my blood and I began heading towards the wharf around midnight, determined to participate in this exciting occupation.

This late night enthusiasm earned me the position of head deckhand almost overnight. I watched, listened, and soon learned the tricks of the trade.

Lazy Man's Cioppino

SERVES 4-6

- *2 lg. fresh crabs*
- *12 each, clams and mussels*
- *2 lbs. shrimp*
- *1 lg. yellow onion*
- *8 garlic cloves*
- *1 bunch Italian flat-leaf parsley*
- *olive oil*

- *½ cup white wine*
- *2 28-oz. cans Italian tomatoes (whole, peeled)*
- *½ cup Italian green olives (pitted)*
- *1 tsp. sugar*
- *salt & black pepper*

Bring a large pot (8 quarts) of salted water to a rapid boil. Carefully drop live crabs into pot. Cook for 15-20 minutes or until done. Remove from water (do not rinse) and cool. Remove crab meat from shell. Remove crab legs, crack gently and remove meat. Cut between knuckles and remove meat. Add crab butter from outer shell to sauce.

You will need a large skillet to prepare remaining ingredients.

Chop onion and garlic coarsely. Remember, the finer the chop the more powerful the flavor. Remove stems from parsley and chop.

Sauté onions, garlic and parsley in olive oil. Add white wine and continue cooking on high heat until onions and garlic are soft. With your hands, squeeze tomatoes into skillet with juice. Add green olives. Add sugar to balance tomato acid. Reduce heat to medium and cook for 10 minutes.

Add clams and mussels and cover skillet. Steam for 6-8 minutes. Add shrimp to skillet 4 minutes after clams and mussels are added. Shake the skillet as you would popcorn to open shells.

Place mussels, clams and shrimp in large serving bowl. Add crab meat. Pour sauce over dish and serve immediately with crusty Italian bread.

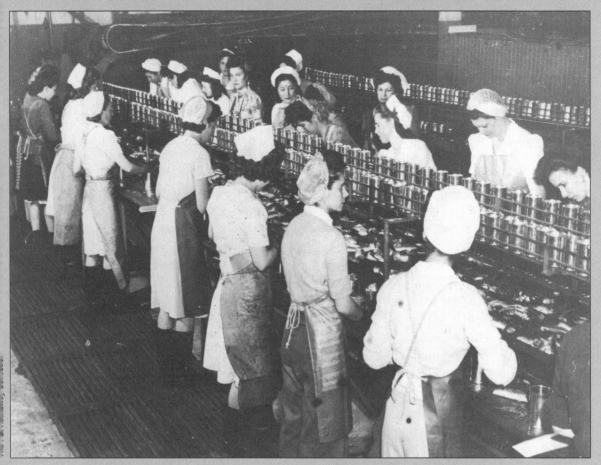

THE SARDINE CANNERIES WERE LARGELY POPULATED BY WOMEN WORKERS. THE ROUTINE WAS HARD, DIRTY AND RELENTLESS. PRIOR TO UNIONIZATION, THESE LADIES WORKED AS LONG AS IT TOOK TO CAN THE ENTIRE CATCH.

Since sardine fishing was done primarily at night, the neighborhood boys and I would wake at the crack of dawn and head for Ocean View Avenue (named Cannery Row in 1958 in honor of John Steinbeck) to watch them unload the evening catch.

It was a sight to see the Row in action as the boats headed towards port. The canneries, over three dozen in their heyday, would blow their whistles and an army of company packers would pour over the hills to work. I am proud to say, my mother was once one of these hard-working women!

PISTO'S SCAMPI

SERVES 4-6

- *12 large, fresh prawns*
- *12-14 large garlic cloves*
- *½ bunch Italian flat-leaf parsley*
- *olive oil*
- *butter*

- *pinch of crushed red pepper*
- *1 lemon (juice only)*
- *½ cup dry white wine*
- *salt & black pepper*

Chop garlic and parsley coarsely and set aside.

Cover the bottom of a large cast iron skillet with an equal amount of olive oil and butter. Pre-heat over high flame. Place fresh, rinsed prawns into hot skillet and season with garlic, red pepper, salt and pepper. Sear prawns approximately 2-3 minutes on each side. Pour lemon juice and ¼ cup white wine over prawns. Add parsley, cover and simmer for 3-5 minutes.

To test for thoroughly cooked prawns, break open at the neck. Look for solid, white meat. Remove prawns from skillet and place on a serving platter.

Add 3 tblsp. butter and 3 tblsp. oil to skillet mixture. Reduce heat and slowly stir in remaining wine. Pour garlic butter sauce over prawns and serve.

THE CREW BREAKS FROM ITS ROUND-THE-CLOCK WORK SCHEDULE FOR LUNCH.

Although my role may not have been very significant , I was proud to be a part of Monterey's fishing heritage.

At quitting time, my buddies and I would hitch a ride up the hill in some unlucky fool's truck, all reeking of the evening catch.

My family was not wealthy, so the bounty of fresh fish I'd managed to claim was always a welcome sight. My mother could cook sardines and rock cod at least 20 different ways.

SICILIAN MARINATED CRAB

SERVES 4-6

- *3 large live or fresh crabs, or 3 fresh, cooked, store-bought crabs*
- *4-6 garlic cloves*
- *½ bunch Italian flat-leaf parsley*
- *1 lemon (juice only)*
- *½ cup olive oil*
- *¼ tsp. ground red pepper*
- *2 tsp. spicy mustard*
- *¼ cup red wine vinegar*
- *salt & freshly ground black pepper*

Bring a large pot (8 quarts) of salted water to a rapid boil. Carefully drop live crabs into pot. Cook for 15-20 minutes. Fresh cooked crabs need not be re-heated.

While the crabs are cooking you may prepare the marinating sauce. You will need a medium-sized mixing bowl. Chop garlic cloves coarsely. Remember, the finer the chop, the more powerful the garlic flavor. Remove stems and chop Italian parsley. Place in bowl. Squeeze lemon juice into bowl. Add vinegar, olive oil, mustard and crushed red pepper. Whisk together. Salt and pepper to taste.

Remove crabs from pot (do not rinse) and let cool until able to handle. Remove outer shell. Remove lungs (fingers) and mouth from shell and discard. Scrape out remaining crab butter. Add crab butter to the marinating sauce.

Remove crab legs. Cut between knuckles for nice serving pieces. Tap each leg gently until cracked. Place on large platter, squeeze lemon juice over crab, and pour sauce over dish. Refrigerate for 1 hour—or as long as you can stand the wait. Serve with crusty sourdough bread and wine (I recommend a light red or a dry white with this dish).

Bibs are recommended.

SICILIAN CRAB PASTA

SERVES 4-6

- *3 lg. live or fresh cooked crabs*
- *1 lb. angel hair pasta*
- *6 garlic cloves*
- *1 lg. yellow onion*
- *olive oil*
- *½ cup sun-dried tomatoes (or soaked, dried)*
- *¼ bunch Italian flat-leaf parsley*
- *2 bunches green onions*
- *6 Roma tomatoes*
- *1 cup Calamata olives (pitted)*
- *¼ tsp. red pepper flakes*
- *½ cup clam juice or white wine*
- *½ lb. butter*
- *1 lemon*
- *salt & black pepper*

Bring a large pot (8 quarts) of salted water to a rapid boil. Carefully drop live crabs into pot. Cook for 15-20 minutes (cooked crabs need not be re-heated).

Remove crabs from pot (do not rinse) and let cool until able to handle. Remove outer shell. Remove lungs (fingers) and mouth from shell and discard. Scrape out remaining crab butter from outer shell to add to sauce. Remove crab legs and crack gently to remove meat. Cut between knuckles and remove meat.

Prepare a 4-quart pot of salted water for pasta. Bring to a rapid boil before adding pasta. Add pasta to boiling water. Cook for 6 minutes, stirring continuously. Do not drain.

You will need a large skillet and a 4-quart pot for remaining ingredients. Chop garlic cloves and onion coarsely. Remember, the finer the chop, the more powerful the flavor. Place in skillet with olive oil and brown. (Soak dried tomatoes in water for 5 minutes to soften.) Remove Italian parsley stems and chop. Chop green onions. Add sun-dried and Roma tomatoes, green onion, parsley, olives, red pepper and clam juice, crab butter or white white and simmer. Add butter. When butter has melted into sauce, fold in crabmeat. Gently mix in pasta. Salt and pepper to taste. Add lemon garnish and serve immediately.

Spicy Clams & Mussels with Pasta

SERVES 4-6

- *24 fresh clams (knocked for freshness)*
- *24 fresh mussels (mixed types optional)*
- *1 lb. fettuccine pasta*
- *6 garlic cloves*
- *1 lg. yellow onion*
- *olive oil*
- *½ bunch Italian flat-leaf parsley*
- *½ bunch fresh basil*
- *2 Andouille sausages or 2 hot Italian sausages*
- *1 cup white wine*
- *2 28-oz. cans Italian tomatoes (whole, peeled)*
- *2 tsp. sugar*
- *¼ tsp. red pepper flakes*
- *3 tsp. Pisto's Sensational Seasoning*
- *1 lemon*
- *salt & black pepper*

Using a 4-quart pot, start water for pasta (4 quarts for each pound of pasta). Add 1 tsp. salt to water. Bring to rapid boil. Add pasta without breaking. Cook for 8 minutes, stirring regularly.

Chop garlic and onion coarsely. Remember, the finer the chop, the more powerful the flavor. Brown onion and garlic in olive oil on high heat. Remove stems from parsley and basil and chop coarsely. Cut sausage into bite-sized pieces. Add parsley, basil and sausage and cook for 10 minutes. Stir in white wine. Boil until liquid is reduced. Squeeze in tomatoes with juice. Add sugar to balance tomato acid, then add red pepper, Sensational Seasoning and stir. Bring to boil for 15 minutes or until sauce is thick. Add clams to sauce and cover skillet. Boil for 2-3 minutes. Add mussels (de-bearded) and boil for 6-8 minutes. Shake the pan, like popcorn, to open shells while cooking.

Drain pasta and place in large serving platter. Arrange clams and mussels on pasta. Pour sauce over dish, salt and pepper to taste and garnish with lemon. Serve immediately.

FAMILY GATHERINGS WERE AN IMPORTANT PART OF OUR LIVES AND WHEN WE GATHERED, GOOD DRINK WAS JUST AS IMPORTANT AS GOOD FOOD. PICTURED HERE ARE A FEW NEIGHBORHOOD BOYS MAKING A LITTLE WINE.

During the summer months, the family would often invite the neighbors over for a traditional Italian feast. Mama would send me down to Troia's Market, where old man Troia would fill my arms with fresh tomatoes, onions and garlic, and send me off with a slap up side the head, saying, "You be a good boy, Johnny."

I would then hurry home, through what is still called "Spaghetti Hill," inviting all those I met on the way home to dinner.

I now own this wine press which serves as the center piece in my garden, among the olive trees, grape vines and lavender.

Rock Fish Chowder

SERVES 4-6

- *4 boned rock fish fillets*
- *1 lg. onion*
- *2 leeks*
- *6 slices thick bacon*
- *10 small red potatoes*
- *1 ear of corn*
- *½ tsp. cayenne pepper*
- *2 tblsp. Worcestershire sauce*
- *1 quart half & half*
- *⅓ cup fresh chopped thyme*
- *salt & black pepper to taste*

Run fingers along fillet to find remaining bones. Pull out bones with small pliers or cut out with a knife.

Cut onion into cubes. Cut leeks down the center then cut into 1½-inch strips. Cut bacon into 1-inch pieces. Cut potatoes into quarters.

Put bacon, onion and leeks into a large pot over high heat. When bacon is fully cooked, remove corn from cob and add to pot. Add cayenne and Worcestershire sauce and stir. Add half & half, thyme and potatoes. Reduce heat to medium, cover and cook for 10 minutes, or until potatoes can be easily pierced with a fork.

Cut fillets into 2-inch cubes and add to pot. Cook over medium heat for 10-12 minutes. Serve with crusty Italian bread.

Rock Fish in Coconut Milk

SERVES 4-6

- *6 boned rock fish fillets*
- *1 lg. yellow onion*
- *2 lg. carrots*
- *1 tsp. fresh ginger*
- *3 jalapeño peppers*
- *½ bunch fresh basil*
- *½ bunch flat-leaf parsley*
- *2 green onions*
- *3 lg. garlic cloves*
- *3 tblsp. peanut oil*
- *2 6-oz. cans coconut milk*
- *4 cups chicken broth*
- *2 tsp. curry powder*
- *1 tsp. Chinese red hot chili oil*
- *2 lemons (juice only)*
- *salt & black pepper*
- *4 cups white rice*

Dice yellow onion, carrots, ginger and peppers. Chop basil, parsley, green onions and garlic coarsely. Pour peanut oil into large pot over high heat. Sauté yellow onions and garlic in pot for 3-5 minutes. Add coconut milk and stir. Add 2 cups of chicken broth, basil, parsley, green onions, carrots, ginger and peppers. Stir in curry powder, hot chili sauce and add remaining broth.

Drop in fillets, cover and poach for 3-5 minutes. Add the juice from lemons, sprinkle with salt and black pepper and simmer for 6-10 minutes.

Steam rice and scoop into individual serving bowls. With a spatula, remove fillets from pot and place over rice. Pour coconut sauce over fish and serve.

Rock Fish Cancun Style

SERVES 2-4

- 1 3-to-4 lb. whole Pacific rock fish (cleaned, scaled, and boned)
- olive oil
- 3 tblsp. mild chili powder
- 1 tblsp. water
- salt & black pepper to taste

- 1 bunch cilantro
- 6 garlic gloves
- 1 lg. yellow onion
- 3 Roma tomatoes
- 1 lemon or lime

To prepare the fish, first cut off fins and split open. Lay the fish belly-up on an oil-coated baking sheet. Salt and pepper fish.

Set oven at 450^0. Mix chili powder with water and 2 tblsp. olive oil to form a thin paste. Paint the fish with the paste. Layer cavity with coarsely chopped cilantro, garlic, onion and cubed tomatoes. Garnish with lemon or lime slices. Bake for 30-40 minutes. Baste and serve hot.

Rock Fish French Style

SERVES 2-4

- 1 3-to-4 lb. Pacific rock fish (cleaned, scaled and boned)
- olive oil
- ¼ cup white wine
- 1 tsp. Pisto's Sensational Seasoning
- 1 med. yellow onion
- ½ bunch flat-leaf parsley

- ¼ bunch fresh basil
- 1 sm. anise bulb
- 6 garlic cloves
- 3 Roma tomatoes
- 1 lemon or lime
- salt & black pepper to taste

Preheat oven to 450^0. To prepare fish, coat with olive oil and wine (including cavity). Place rock fish on an oiled baking sheet.

Sprinkle Sensational Seasoning and salt and pepper into cavity. Chop onion into rings. Chop parsley, basil, anise and garlic coarsely. Fill fish cavity with onion, parsley, and anise leaving enough garlic, onion and parsley to generously season the outer body of fish. Slice lemon or lime into thin rings. Cut tomatoes into small cubes. Cover fish with lemon or lime rings, tomatoes, garlic, onion and parsley. Bake for 30-40 minutes or until done. Serve with pan juices.

ROCK FISH IN PARCHMENT

SERVES 2

- *2 lg. boned rock fish fillets*
- *1 green zucchini*
- *1 yellow zucchini*
- *1-3 oz. white wine*
- *6-8 snow pea pods*

- *¼ bunch fresh basil*
- *4 cloves of garlic*
- *olive oil*
- *1 lg. Roma tomato*
- *2 tsp. butter*

- *2 24"-x-24" sheets parchment*
- *2 tblsp. Pisto's Sensational Seasoning*
- *1 lemon*
- *salt & black pepper to taste*

Cut zucchini into bite-sized wedges. Remove juice and seeds from tomato. Cut tomato meat into bite-sized pieces. Remove stems from peas and basil. Chop garlic coarsely.

Pre-heat oven to 350⁰. Paint parchment paper thoroughly with olive oil on both sides. Place on large baking pan.

Paint fillets with olive oil on both sides. Sprinkle with Sensational Seasoning. Place mixed vegetables and basil in the center of the parchment and season with salt and pepper. Place fish on vegetables. Cut lemon into rounds and place on fillets. Add butter and wine. Fold parchment over, covering fish and twist parchment ends and tops closed. Bake for 20-30 minutes or until done. Serve in parchment.

ROCK FISH WITH PASTA

SERVES 4

- *2 boned rock fish fillets*
- *1 lb. spaghetti pasta*
- *1 med. yellow onion*
- *½ bunch flat-leaf parsley*
- *½ bunch fresh basil*
- *¼ cup fennel*

- *2 med. Roma tomatoes*
- *3 lg. garlic cloves*
- *olive oil*
- *12 pitted Calamata olives*
- *1 tblsp. capers*
- *1 tsp. Pisto's Sensational Seasoning*

- *¼ cup white wine*
- *½ tsp. cayenne pepper*
- *pinch saffron*
- *3 cups water*
- *salt & black pepper*

Chop onion, parsley, fennel and basil coarsely. Dice tomatoes. Crush garlic cloves. Set aside a small amount of the basil and parsley for garnish.

In a large pot, sauté onion in olive oil for 3 minutes over high heat. Add garlic, tomatoes, parsley, fennel and basil, olives, capers, and white wine. Reduce heat to medium and sauté for 5 minutes. Add cayenne, Sensational Seasoning, saffron, and salt and pepper. Slowly stir in water. Drop in fillets and cover 3/4 of pot to poach fish for 4-6 minutes or until done. When boiling, add pasta broken into 3-4 inch sections and stir. Cover and boil for 2-4 minutes. Pour into serving bowl and garnish with parsley and basil. This dish is meant to be soupy and juicy.

A FISHING BOAT DRESSED FOR THE CELEBRATION HONORING THE PATRON SAINT OF FISHERMEN, SANTA ROSALITA.

I talians have always been deeply religious, and they brought their beliefs and customs with them to Monterey. These customs include Monterey's popular Santa Rosalita Festival, which brings us together to honor the patron saint of fishermen.

THIS FAMOUS PHOTOGRAPH DEPICTS CANNERY ROW IN ITS HEYDAY, WITH OVER 30 CANNERIES IN OPERATION, CIRCA 1948.   PHOTO BY G. ROBINSON

The Pat Hathaway Collection

Ocean View Avenue, pictured here at the peak of the sardine boom, was constantly changing, with canneries and honky tonks coming and going.

Little did we know then that it would soon earn its place in history as Steinbeck's Cannery Row, attracting tourists from all over the world.

CALAMARI/SQUID

Calamari St. Tropez • Calamari with
Pasta & Marinara • Calamari in Ink
Sauce • Calamari Stuffing in Vegetable
Boats • Stuffed Calamari • Squid
Cioppino • Abalonetti's World Famous
Marty's Special • Calamari Doré •
Sicilian Squid Salad

CALAMARI ST. TROPEZ

SERVES 4

- 2½ lbs. cleaned squid mantles & tentacles
- 1 lg. yellow onion
- 3 carrots
- 3 leeks (white portion only)
- 2 lg. potatoes
- 6 Roma tomatoes
- 4 garlic cloves
- ½ tsp. dried basil
- rinds from ½ lemon & ½ orange
- ¼ cup Ricard liquor (optional)
- ½ cup white wine
- 2 tblsp. tomato paste
- 2 tblsp. Pisto's Sensational Seasoning
- pinch of saffron
- olive oil
- salt & black pepper to taste

Dice onion. Cut carrots and leeks into matchstick-sized pieces. Cut potatoes into ½-inch slices. Chop tomatoes into bite-sized pieces. Dice garlic.

Using a 4-quart pot, sauté onions, leeks, potatoes, carrots, garlic and basil in olive oil for 5-7 minutes over medium heat. Add lemon and orange rinds, Ricard liquor, white wine, tomatoes and tomato paste, stirring continuously. Stir in Sensational Seasoning, saffron, and salt and black pepper. Cover and cook for 10 minutes.

Cut squid mantles into rings. Sauté rings and tentacles in a large skillet with olive oil and a splash of white wine for 3-5 minutes. Mix into sauce and serve with toasted Italian bread.

TO ME, THIS PHOTOGRAPH OF A LONE FISHERMAN REPRESENTS THE DEDICATION TO THE TRADE INBRED IN THE ITALIAN TRADITION.

There is a certain feeling—a state of mind—you acquire as a fisherman. It's a feeling you get whether you are young or old, a seasoned sportsman, or a weekend fisherman. Although I don't have as much time for fishing as I used to, these experiences will be with me for the rest of my days.

It starts with anticipating the catch. Like a treasure hunter, you never know what the prize will be. When I was young, I spent many a day fishing from the pier.

As I would search for the perfect spot to cast my line, the moist fog still hanging low to the ground, I would calculate the depth of the water, and the space I would allow the other thrillseekers on the pier.

Once situated, I would become "The Old Man of the Sea," carefully baiting my line, casting my pole and dreaming of the "Big One." As I gazed into the waters of the bay, I would contemplate my existence and that of my prey. Startled by a tug on the line, the thrills would begin. Even if I went home empty handed, I always felt I had acquired, at least, peace of mind.

CALAMARI WITH PASTA & MARINARA

SERVES 4-6

- *1 lb. cleaned squid mantles & tentacles*
- *Marinara sauce (recipe pg. 66)*
- *½ lb. penné pasta*
- *1 med. yellow onion*
- *½ cup pitted Calamata olives*
- *¼ bunch fresh basil*
- *¼ bunch Italian flat-leaf parsley*

- *4 garlic cloves*
- *2 lg. Roma tomatoes*
- *¼ cup capers*
- *½ tsp. red pepper flakes*
- *½ cup red wine*
- *salt & black pepper to taste*

Prepare marinara sauce.

Cook pasta in 3 quarts rapidly boiling, salted water. To prepare al denté, test after 7 minutes. Do not overcook.

Chop onion, olives, basil, parsley and garlic coarsely. Cut tomatoes into small cubes. Cut cleaned squid mantles into rings.

In a large skillet, sauté onion and garlic for 2 minutes. Add capers, tomatoes, olives, basil, parsley, red and black pepper. Add squid rings and tentacles and continue to sauté for 2-3 minutes. Stir in red wine and simmer for 5 minutes. Serve hot.

EDWARD FLANDERS ROBB "DOC" RICKETTS.

MADAME FLORA WOODS.

E d "Doc" Ricketts was John Steinbeck's friend and co-author of the book *Sea of Cortez*. Doc was a resident of Cannery Row, living out of his biological lab on old Ocean View Avenue. Although Doc's work had a major impact on modern marine biology, he was a shy and quiet man. Steinbeck immortalized him and his neighbor, Flora Woods, in the famous little book about Ocean View Avenue Steinbeck titled *Cannery Row*.

By the late forties, it seemed Cannery Row's days were numbered. Its demise became obvious on that fateful day in May of 1948, when Doc passed on to that great lab in the sky, just three days before his 51st birthday. He was hit while crossing the railroad tracks by the old Del Monte Express. News of his untimely death traveled fast, as it does in small towns. I remember it was a sad day, even for those who never knew him.

A lthough Flora Woods saved many poor souls over the years with her kind acts and charitable donations, her occupation as madame of a house of ill repute made the God-fearing people of Monterey shun her like the plague. She died penniless in August of 1948.

Her Lone Star Cafe was the Row's most notorious bordello. Not only was it popular with local workers and visitors, but later we found it had also served the local gentry.

After her death, the Lone Star became a warehouse for the remaining canneries, which would later burn to the ground. I must say, I was much too young to have seen these goings-on myself.

Squid Cleaning Instructions

Easy cleaning instructions:

1) Holding the mantle in one hand, pinch pen (transparent backbone) with index finger and thumb of opposite hand, separating pen from mantle;

2) Gently pull pen out of mantle, easing viscera out along with pen;

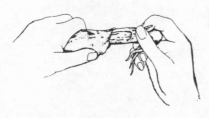

Continued on next page

CALAMARI IN INK SAUCE

SERVES 4

- *3 lbs. fresh, whole squid, bagged in its own ink*
- *2 med. yellow onions*
- *5 garlic cloves*
- *olive oil*
- *3 tblsp. tomato paste*
- *¼ cup red wine*
- *2 oz. Ricard liquor (optional)*
- *½ bunch Italian flat-leaf parsley (chopped coarsely)*
- *pinch of crushed red pepper*
- *salt & black pepper to taste*

Call your favorite fishmonger a day in advance and ask him to set aside a few pounds of the next morning's catch of squid in its own ink. Clean squid, saving all liquid, mantles and tentacles. Cut mantles into rings and set aside while you prepare other ingredients.

Dice onions and garlic. Sauté onions and garlic in olive oil. When lightly browned, add tomato paste and simmer over medium heat for 8 minutes, stirring continuously. Add wine and Ricard and cook for 5 more minutes. Add squid rings, heads and its dark inky liquid and stir. Cook for 5-10 minutes, until the mixture has the consistency of stew. Do not overcook or squid will taste like rubber. Add chopped parsley, salt, black and red pepper and serve.

CALAMARI STUFFING IN VEGETABLE BOATS

SERVES 4

- 1½ lbs. squid, cleaned
- olive oil
- ½ cup white wine
- 3 cups bread crumbs
- ¼ bunch flat-leaf parsley
- ¼ bunch fresh basil

- 1 tsp. dried thyme
- ½ cup Reggiano cheese
- ½ cup raisins
- 2 eggs
- black pepper

Choose one or more of these vegetables to make 8 serving boats:

—lg. red, yellow, & green peppers
—lg. yellow onions
—lg. green & yellow zucchinis

—lg. tomatoes
—bell peppers
—med. eggplant

Scrape out the center of the vegetables of your choice, leaving anywhere from ¼-inch to ½-inch of meat. Reserve meat for filling. Always cut eggplant and zucchini length-wise. Begin your onion boat by removing the first layer of skin and cutting off the root end. Slowly bore through the layers with a spoon. Also note, tomatoes can be messy if they are not firm.

Chop vegetable meat coarsely. In a medium frying pan, sauté the filling in olive oil. Add white wine and continue cooking for 10 minutes over high heat.

In a mixing bowl, soak bread crumbs in ½ cup water for 2 minutes and drain. Blend the squid in a cuisinart food processor for approximately 1 minute. Pour into a mixing bowl. Chop parsley and basil coarsely. Add parsley, basil, thyme, black pepper, cheese, raisins and eggs to mixing bowl and stir. Squeeze excess water from bread crumbs, then add to the squid mixture. Add the sautéed vegetables and mix well. Stuff this mixture into vegetable boats. Place vegetables in a baking pan. Cover the bottom of the pan with ¼-inch of water. Bake in a pre-heated 350⁰-oven for approximately 1 hour.

Continued from last page

Squid Cleaning

3) Cut away tentacles in front of eyes;

4) Squeeze tentacles near cut end to pop out hard, chitinous beak. Discard beak, pen, and viscera. Reserve mantle and tentacles;

Continued on next page

Continued from last page

Squid Cleaning

5) Scrape membrane to loosen from mantle. Peel away all membranes and discard. Rinse mantle thoroughly with cold water to remove any remaining viscera, pat dry;

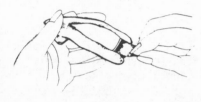

6) Use mantle whole or cut into rings. Use tentacles in recipes, or fry and serve as an appetizer.

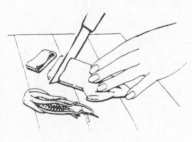

STUFFED CALAMARI

SERVES 4

- *12 cleaned squid mantles and tentacles*
- *1½ lbs. country sausage*
- *Marinara sauce (recipe pg. 66)*
- *olive oil*
- *1 lg. yellow onion*
- *½ cup raisins*
- *½ cup pine nuts*
- *1 cup seasoned bread crumbs*
- *1 tsp. Pisto's Sensational Seasoning*
- *1 egg*

Prepare traditional marinara sauce.

Mince sausage. Chop onion and squid tentacles fine. In a large, oiled skillet, sauté sausage, onion, raisins, pine nuts, and squid tentacles for 10 minutes, until sausage is fully cooked. Drain fat. Place cooked ingredients in mixing bowl. Add bread crumbs and Sensational Seasoning and stir. Moisten with 2 tblsp. of water. Add egg. Mix until ingredients can be molded like meatloaf.

Stuff squid mantles with mixture and close ends with toothpicks. Prick squid 3 to 4 times with a fork to remove excess liquid from filling.

Add squid to marinara sauce and cook for 10 minutes. Cover and continue cooking for 5 minutes. Pull squid out and remove toothpicks. Cut mantles into three sections and serve with sauce.

JOHN STEINBECK, THE TALENTED AND MEMORABLE AUTHOR WHO MADE CANNERY ROW FAMOUS.

By 1949, with the sardines virtually gone, the canneries began to close. Steinbeck's Cannery Row would soon be gone forever.

Many fishermen found themselves looking for other types of work, while others simply went back to fishing for salmon or squid. In memory of those days, I would like to share this quote from the book *Cannery Row:*

Cannery Row in Monterey in California is a poem, a stink, a grating noise, a quality of light, a tone, a habit, a nostalgia, a dream. Cannery Row is the gathered and scattered, tin and iron and rust and splintered wood, chipped pavement and weedy lots and junk heaps, sardine canneries of corrugated iron, honky tonks, restaurants and whore houses, and little crowded groceries, and laboratories and flophouses.

SQUID CIOPPINO

SERVES 4

- 2 lbs. cleaned, whole squid
- 2 lg. potatoes
- 2 carrots
- 4 stalks celery
- 1 med. yellow onion
- 4 garlic cloves
- olive oil
- ¼ bunch Italian flat-leaf parsley

- ½ cup pitted, green olives
- 3 tblsp. capers
- 1 cup white wine
- 1 tsp. Pisto's Sensational Seasoning
- 1 28-oz. can whole, peeled tomatoes
- ½ tsp. red pepper flakes
- salt & black pepper to taste

Peel potatoes and carrots. Cut celery, potatoes and carrots into bite-sized pieces. Chop onion and garlic coarsely. Cover bottom of a 1-quart pot with olive oil. Heat over medium flame.

Add potatoes, carrots, celery, onion, parsley, olives, capers and garlic. Sauté for 12-15 minutes. Add white wine and Sensational Seasoning. Cook for 5 minutes to reduce wine. Add tomatoes with juice and stir. Add red pepper, salt and black pepper. As tomato sauce reduces, add water, keeping a 1-inch level of liquid in pot. Cook until potatoes can be pierced with a fork. Cut squid into rings and tentacles. Stir in squid. Cover and cook for 8-10 minutes. Your cioppino is now ready to serve.

ABALONETTI'S WORLD FAMOUS MARTY'S SPECIAL

SERVES 6

- 18 squid fillets
- 2-3 eggplants
- Marinara sauce (recipe, pg. 66)
- olive oil
- ¼ cup Parmesan cheese

- salt & black pepper to taste
- 2 eggs
- 2 cups bread crumbs
- 2 tsp. Pisto's Sensational Seasoning

Prepare eggplant by cutting into thin slices (about ¼-inch thick). Salt each slice lightly and let stand for 30 minutes to leach out bitterness (this step is optional). Wipe with a dry towel.

Prepare marinara sauce. Brush eggplant with olive oil and season with salt and pepper. Using a stovetop grill or conventional oven, grill or bake for 6-8 minutes, until lightly browned and soft. Place bread crumbs in a mixing bowl. Mix in Pisto's Sensational Seasoning. Prepare eggs in separate mixing bowl. Beat eggs with 2 tblsp. water. Dip squid in egg batter then into bread crumbs. Cover the bottom of a large skillet with olive oil. Heat over medium flame. When oil is hot, place squid in skillet. Grill until brown on each side. Place eggplant in serving platter. Top each eggplant with 3 squid fillets each. Cover with marinara sauce. Bake for 15-20 minutes. Garnish with cheese and serve hot.

THE HEROES OF MY TIME GATHERING FOR A GAME OF CARDS.

PHOTO BY WM. L. MORGAN

We would sit for hours on "The Row," listening attentively to the tales of just a few years past, when these fishermen were the kings of the sea, with catches unmatched anywhere in the world.

With those days behind them, they spent their time playing cards, and betting on the size of the day's catch, while the few remaining workers passed by. Nobody seemed to notice the stench of rotting fish.

CALAMARI DORÉ

SERVES 6

- *12 cleaned squid fillets*
- *1 lemon (zest & juice)*
- *2 cups flour*
- *1 tsp. fresh chopped parsley*
- *salt & black pepper to taste*

- *2 eggs*
- *2 tblsp. water*
- *olive oil*
- *2 tblsp. butter*

Peel 2 tblsp. of zest from lemon and place in bowl. Mix in flour, parsley, salt and pepper. Prepare egg batter in separate mixing bowl by beating eggs with 2 tblsp. water. Dip squid in flour then into egg, then back into the flour and into the egg.

In a non-stick skillet (a pancake grill works great) set over a high heat, add olive oil and butter. When hot, add 3-4 fillets at a time. Cook for 1-2 minutes on each side. Squeeze fresh lemon juice over fillets and serve. Optional: you may use a slightly smaller pan as a press to keep squid from curling.

SICILIAN SQUID SALAD

SERVES 4-6

- *1½ lbs. cleaned, whole squid*
- *salt to taste*
- *4 garlic cloves*
- *¼ bunch Italian flat-leaf parsley*
- *½ cup pitted Calamata olives*

- *4 tblsp. red wine vinegar*
- *1½ lemons (juice only)*
- *3 tblsp. capers*
- *olive oil*
- *1 tblsp. Pisto's Sensational Seasoning*

Bring a 1-gallon pot of salted water to rapid boil. Add squid and cook for 3-5 minutes. Drain and place in serving bowl.

Finely chop garlic, coarsely chop parsley. Cut olives in half. Add vinegar, lemon juice, olive oil, capers, parsley, garlic, and Pisto's Seasoning. Stir and serve.

THE FISHING BOAT *CATRINA*, OWNED BY THE DIMAGGIO FAMILY, CIRCA 1910.

By the late 1950s, most of Monterey's fishermen were staking their fortunes on squid in between making jaunts to Alaska. Just as in the days of the sardines, the action occurred at night. Most of the canneries were gone, so the small family fishermen were on their own.

For several years I worked on the fishing boat *Catrina*, hauling in our fair share of anchovies, mackerel and squid.

We would sell our catch to the local cannery and restaurants on and around the wharf.

Thanks to my father, I was always decently dressed. When I would walk down the wharf to sell my catch, the boys would yell out, "Hey, Johnny, where'd you get those spiffy dress pants?"

To this day, I believe it was those "spiffy dress pants" that landed me my first job in the restaurant business.

A ROUTINE FIRE CALL ON CANNERY ROW.

PHOTO BY WM. L. MORGAN

It was in December of 1951 when the first fire on old Ocean View Avenue broke out. Said to be the largest food industry fire in the country's history at the time, the former Del Mar Cannery burned to the ground. This set off a chain reaction and the canneries burned, one by one, for almost ten years. The fire alarms were such a regular occurrence that residents just shook their heads and said, "There goes another stinkin' cannery." I'm sure it caused havoc with the insurance companies, since the fires were all quite mysterious.

Today you will find a new Cannery Row. The smell in the air is no longer that of rotting fish, but rather that of smoked salmon and hamburgers. Where the canneries once stood, you will find a collection of gift shops and restaurants. The packers have been replaced by tourists looking for a glimpse of Steinbeck's Cannery Row. And we "old timers" hang around for an opportunity to share these memories with anyone who will listen.

MEAT, POULTRY & WILD GAME

Red Pepper Steak • Green Peppercorn Steak • Barbecue Porterhouse or Tri-Tip • Grilled Rib Eye or New York Steak • Filet Mignon in Mushroom Sauce • Barbecue Beef Filet • Roundbone Shoulder Lamb Chops • Pisto's Rack of Lamb with Mint Sauce • Brick Chicken • Chicken Rollatini • Breaded Rabbit • Quail in White Wine Sauce • Pheasant & Quail Stew • Holiday Quail with Orange Glaze

RED PEPPER STEAK

SERVES 2

- 2 16-oz. New York steaks
- ¼ cup whole black peppercorns
- ¼ cup whole red peppercorns
- salt to taste
- 1 tsp. garlic powder
- ¼ cup red wine
- 1 tsp. butter

Crush peppercorns to a coarse consistency. Pour into pie pan. Add salt and garlic powder and mix. Press steaks into mixture, coating both sides heavily.

Pre-heat cast iron skillet for 10 minutes on medium-high heat. Place steaks in smoking skillet and cook until seared (approximately 4-6 minutes on each side) for medium rare meat. Remove from skillet and cover with foil to keep warm.

To make pepper sauce, de-glaze skillet with wine. Reduce, then add butter and stir. Remove foil from meat and place on individual plates. Pour sauce over steaks and serve.

GREEN PEPPERCORN STEAK

SERVES 2

- 2 16-oz. New York steaks
- ¼ cup green peppercorns in brine
- salt & black pepper to taste
- 4 tblsp. Pisto's Sensational Seasoning
- ½ cup beef stock or bouillon cubes
- ¼ cup finely chopped shallots
- ¼ cup brandy
- ½ cup beef stock or bouillon cube & water
- ¼ cup heavy cream
- 1 tsp. butter

Pre-heat cast iron skillet for 10 minutes on medium-high heat. Crush half of the peppercorns to a coarse consistency, leaving the rest whole. Salt and pepper steak, then coat with Sensational Seasoning on both sides.

Place meat in smoking skillet and cook for approximately 3-5 minutes per side for medium rare meat. Remove meat from skillet and cover with foil to keep warm.

De-glaze skillet with beef stock or bouillon to make the sauce. Add chopped shallots and stir. Add brandy and peppercorns with brine and stir. Add cream and stir until sauce thickens. Then add butter and stir until melted. Remove foil and slice steak ⅛-inch to ¼-inch thick at an angle and place on individual plates. Pour sauce over meat and serve.

BARBECUED PORTERHOUSE OR TRI-TIP

SERVES 2

- 2½ lbs. tri-tip cut or porterhouse steaks
- 2 tblsp. garlic powder
- salt & pepper to taste
- olive oil
- 4 tblsp. Sensational Seasoning

Trim thick portions of fat from tri-tip cut. Paint meat with olive oil on all sides. Sprinkle meat with garlic powder, salt, pepper and Sensational Seasoning. Pat seasoning into meat before placing on grill. Note: season meat immediately prior to barbecuing to avoid blanching its juices.

When barbecue coals are white hot, place meat fat side down on grill. Cook uncovered for approximately 3-5 minutes, then turn. Cover grill with top vent half open and bottom vent wide open. Barbecue approximately 6 minutes on each side for medium rare meat, longer for thick cuts. Remove meat from grill and serve. Tri-tip steak should be sliced in ⅛-inch to ¼-inch slices at an angle.

GRILLED RIB EYE OR NEW YORK STEAK

SERVES 2

- 2 1"-thick rib eye or New York steak
- 2 tblsp. garlic powder
- salt & pepper to taste
- olive oil
- 4 tblsp. Sensational Seasoning

Pre-heat cast iron stovetop grill approximately 10 minutes on medium heat or until smoking (or use traditional barbecue).

Paint meat with olive oil on both sides. Sprinkle garlic powder, salt, pepper and Sensational Seasoning on both sides of meat. Pat seasonings onto meat before placing on grill. Note: season meat immediately prior to barbecuing to avoid blanching its juices.

Grill meat uncovered approximately 6 minutes on each side for medium rare meat, longer for thicker pieces. Remove meat from grill and serve.

FILET MIGNON IN MUSHROOM SAUCE

SERVES 2

- *2 ¾"-filet mignon medallions*
- *olive oil*
- *1 sm. shallot*
- *¼ bunch flat-leaf parsley*
- *4 garlic cloves*

- *2 cups asst. wild mushrooms*
- *1 tblsp. sherry*
- *¼ cup beef stock or bouillon*
- *¼ cup cognac or brandy*
- *salt & black pepper to taste*

- *¼ cup heavy cream*
- *2 tblsp. Dijon mustard*

Pour olive oil in saucepan and heat over medium flame. Chop shallots, parsley and garlic coarsely. Add sliced mushrooms and sauté for 8-10 minutes. Add to saucepan and stir.

Add sherry and salt and pepper. Simmer for 15 minutes or until liquid has evaporated. Pre-heat cast iron skillet for 10 minutes on medium heat. It should be very hot. Salt and pepper meat. Place medallions in the hot skillet and cook for approximately 2-3 minutes on each side for rare to medium rare meat. Remove medallions and de-glaze skillet with beef stock or bouillon.

Slowly add shallots, cognac or brandy, *being aware that it may ignite*. Reduce heat slightly before adding the cream and mustard. Stir until mixture thickens. Place medallions on a bed of mushrooms. Pour the remaining sauce over medallions and serve.

BARBECUE BEEF FILET

SERVES 6-8

- *whole beef filet (de-nude and remove fat)*
- *3 tblsp. garlic powder*
- *salt & pepper to taste*

- *olive oil*
- *6 tblsp. Pisto's Sensational Seasoning*

Paint meat with olive oil on all sides. Sprinkle with garlic powder, salt, pepper and Pisto's Sensational Seasoning. Pat seasoning onto meat before placing on the grill. Note: season your meat immediately before barbecuing to avoid blanching its juices.

When barbecue coals are white hot, place meat on grill. Cook for 3-5 minutes uncovered. Cover, leaving top air vent half-open, and bottom vent open wide. Barbecue approximately 6-8 minutes or until done. Remove from grill and slice meat at an angle into thin cuts and serve. Best served very rare.

ROUNDBONE SHOULDER LAMB CHOPS

SERVES 4

- *4 shoulder lamb chops*
- *6 garlic cloves*
- *1 cup white wine*
- *¼ tsp. dried thyme*
- *½ tsp. Pisto's Sensational Seasoning*

Coarsely chop garlic cloves. Place lamb chops in medium-size dish with garlic, white wine, thyme and Sensational Seasoning. Marinate chops for a minimum of 1 hour before cooking. Prepare barbeque and when coals are white hot, grill for approximately 6 minutes on first side and 10 minutes on second side or until done.

❖

PISTO'S RACK OF LAMB WITH MINT SAUCE

SERVES 4-6

- *2 racks of lamb*
- *olive oil*
- *aluminum foil*
- *¼ cup Sensational Seasoning*
- *1 cup seasoned bread crumbs*
- *¼ cup Dijon mustard*
- *salt & black pepper to taste*

Pre-heat oven to 450⁰. Pre-heat cast iron skillet for 10 minutes on highest heat. While the skillet is heating up, cover the exposed bones of the lamb with tin foil. Paint rack with oil, rub in Sensational Seasoning, salt and pepper. Place in smoking hot skillet and brown 3 minutes on each side. Remove meat from skillet.

Coat meat with mustard. Sprinkle bread crumbs on mustard. Cook in pre-heated oven for approximately 15-20 minutes for rare to medium rare meat. Serve with mint sauce.

MINT SAUCE

- *1 cup fresh mint*
- *6 garlic cloves*
- *salt & pepper to taste*
- *½ cup red wine vinegar*
- *2 tblsp. sugar*

Dice mint, chop garlic coarsely. Warm all ingredients in skillet for 2-3 minutes and serve.

BRICK CHICKEN

SERVES 4

- 4 boneless chicken breasts
- 2 foil-covered bricks
- olive oil
- 10 garlic cloves
- 2 tsp. Sensational Seasoning
- ¼ cup vermouth
- 1 tsp. butter
- 2 tsp. dry oregano
- 2 lg. lemons

You will need an extra-large cast iron skillet and a second pan, large enough to hold 2 bricks yet small enough to fit inside the large skillet, to be used as a press (this pan's bottom must be clean or covered with foil). Cover bottom of first skillet with oil and whole garlic cloves. Heat over medium flame for approximately 5 minutes. Season chicken with Sensational Seasoning, then place in prepared skillet. Cover with second pan and weigh it down with bricks. Cook approximately 8-10 minutes, over medium heat on each side or until done. Transfer chicken from skillet to serving plate and cover. Add vermouth, butter, oregano and juice from lemons to skillet and stir until sauce is slightly reduced. Pour sauce over chicken and serve.

CHICKEN ROLLATINI

SERVES 4

- 4 boneless, skinned chicken breasts
- olive oil
- salt & black pepper to taste
- ½ cup seasoned bread crumbs
- 2 tblsp. raisins
- 2 tblsp. pine nuts
- 4 thin slices prosciutto
- 4 green onions (cut into 2" pieces)
- 2 tblsp. butter
- ¼ cup white wine
- 3 garlic cloves (chopped fine)
- 3 tblsp. flat-leaf parsley (chopped)

Pound chicken breasts with wooden mallet, until breasts double in size (using wax paper to cover chicken breasts). Brush chicken with olive oil and season with salt and pepper. Mix bread crumbs with pine nuts, raisins and 2 tblsp. of olive oil. Top each breast with slice of proscuitto, 2 tblsp. of bread crumb mixture and 3 pieces of green onions. Then roll up chicken and fasten with toothpick. Pre-heat skillet over medium-high flame with 2 tblsp. of butter and olive oil. When butter has melted add chicken, salt and pepper. Cook for 12-15 minutes, turning chicken as it browns.

Transfer chicken from skillet to serving plate. Add 2 tblsp. of butter and chopped garlic to skillet. Sauté for 2 minutes, then de-glaze pan with wine. When wine begins to reduce stir in chopped parsley and remove from heat. Pour sauce over chicken and serve.

MY FAVORITE UNCLE, GAETANO CAMPAGNO, AND HIS WIFE, MARIA.

Immigrating was not for the meek. My relatives, who came directly from Sicily, had a rough time. The biggest problem they faced when coming to America was the language barrier.

My uncle Gaetano's story is as sweet as apple pie. Summoned to Monterey by family and friends, he embarked upon his journey knowing just a few English words, which included, apple pie and coffee.

Slow to pick up the language of his new homeland, he actually subsisted for days on coffee and apple pie.

Uncle Gaetano was hardworking and had a genuine love for the human race. Throughout his life he spoke in broken English. In spite of this obstacle, he managed to carry on in-depth conversations with his eyes. He taught me to appreciate the lives of others and the harvests from the land and sea around us.

My uncle owned a fish truck and for over thirty years he would rise at dawn and head to the wharf, where he would buy fresh fish from Monterey's fishermen. He would peddle the catch at homes and farms throughout the county, sometimes for cash, most often for chickens, pigs, goats, produce and other commodities.

BREADED RABBIT

SERVES 4

- 1 whole rabbit (cut in pieces)
- ½ cup dried wild mushrooms
- 2 cups flour
- 4 tsp. Pisto's Sensational Seasoning
- 3 tblsp. butter or margarine
- olive oil
- 2 garlic cloves, chopped coarsely
- 1½ cups diced celery
- 1½ cups diced carrots
- 1½ cups diced onions
- ½ cup pitted Calamata olives
- ½ cup white wine
- pinch of saffron
- salt & black pepper to taste

Soak mushrooms in water for 30 minutes before using (to reconstitute). Squeeze water from mushrooms and chop coarsely.

Mix flour, Sensational Seasoning, salt and pepper in a pie pan. Coat rabbit with flour mixture.

Cover the bottom of a brazing pan with butter and olive oil. Place pan over high heat. When pan is hot, add rabbit. When rabbit begins to brown evenly, reduce heat and cook for approximately 20 minutes, turning the rabbit on all sides to brown.

Remove rabbit from pan. In its place, add the garlic, celery, carrots, onions and chopped mushrooms and stir. Add olives, white wine, saffron, salt and pepper. You may add a bit of the water from the mushrooms for flavor. (Don't use the residue that has accumulated on the bottom.)

Simmer for 5 minutes, stirring occasionally. Return rabbit to the pan. Cover and cook over medium heat for about 30 minutes or until done. Serve rabbit with vegetables on the side.

THICK FOG SETTLES OVER SALINAS VALLEY IN THE EARLY MORNING.

Often I would travel with Uncle Gaetano on these daily adventures. Starting at the crack of dawn, we would head down to the wharf to pick up the morning's catch. After securing the load we would head out to the valley to sell our wares. I remember the sounds of our teeth chattering from the cold morning air.

The valley dwellers would meet us at their property line to make their selections of the day.

Many of these shoppers didn't speak English any better than my uncle. They were Portuguese, Spanish and Mexican, all claiming their stakes in what was to become the nation's "Salad Bowl."

QUAIL IN WHITE WINE SAUCE

SERVES 4

- *8 fresh quail, semi-boned*
- *1½ cups white wine*
- *olive oil*
- *8 garlic cloves, chopped coarsely*

- *4 tblsp. Pisto's Sensational Seasoning*
- *4 tsp. balsamic vinegar*
- *salt & black pepper to taste*

Butterfly quail. Marinate quail in 1 cup of white wine, 3 tblsp. olive oil, and 4 cloves of chopped garlic for 15 minutes.

Pre-heat cast iron skillet for 10 minutes on medium heat. Sprinkle quail with Sensational Seasoning and place on grill, skin side down and brown approximately 2-3 minutes on each side. Remove quail from skillet.

Pre-heat oven to 400⁰. Cover the bottom of a baking dish with ½ cup white wine. Place quail in baking dish skin side up. Bake for approximately 10 minutes or until done.

In a medium frying pan, sauté remaining garlic in olive oil over high heat. Add balsamic vinegar, salt and pepper. Pour ¼ cup of quail juice from the baking dish into the frying pan and stir until the mixture reduces to a syrup.

Pour the syrup over quail and serve.

VALLEY DWELLER FEEDING HER CHICKENS AT ONE OF MONTEREY COUNTY'S EARLY HOMESTEADS.

Often these settlers would bring produce, poultry and livestock to trade for my uncle's fish. One such trade will stick in my mind forever. Every Tuesday this sweet lady would meet the truck. Uncle Gaetano would trade fish for her chickens. Her sight was failing and my uncle knew this. One morning she arrived with a dozen of her chickens following close behind and asked to make a trade. My uncle winked at me as he began to strike the deal.

"I will give you a nice big fish for those four chickens there," he said. She nodded and began to walk away, leaving all her chickens behind. As I began gathering up the twelve chickens, I could see my uncle was struggling with his faith. "Wait," he said to me with his head hung low. "Let them go—all of them." The chickens scurried to catch up with their maid, who never knew of the deal she really got. My uncle, through such actions, also taught me to be honest and humble.

PHEASANT & QUAIL STEW

SERVES 6-8

- 1 med.-sized sectioned pheasant
- 6 quail (semi-boned)
- 3 sprigs rosemary
- ½ cup dried porcini mushrooms
- 6 garlic cloves
- ¼ bunch Italian flat-leaf parsley
- 1 med. yellow onion
- salt & pepper to taste

- 2 cups white wine
- olive oil
- 2 med. carrots
- 2 lg. leeks
- 1 16-oz. can chopped Italian tomatoes
- ¼ tsp. cracked red pepper
- 1 cup chicken broth or bouillon

Marinate pheasant and quail in white wine, rosemary sprigs and salt and pepper for 1 hour. Soak mushrooms in ½ cup water for 20 minutes to reconstitute.

Chop garlic, onion and parsley coarsely. Cover bottom of a large cast iron skillet with olive oil. Pre-heat cast iron skillet for 10 minutes on medium heat. When the skillet is hot add pheasant and quail and brown.

Remove birds from skillet and in its place add garlic, onions, leeks, carrots, parsley and drained mushrooms. Sauté over medium heat until onions and garlic soften. Pour in wine marinade and stir. Add tomatoes, salt, red and black pepper and mix. Stir in chicken broth.

Return birds to skillet, with the larger pieces on the bottom, and bring ingredients to a boil. Reduce heat to medium and simmer for approximately 30 minutes or until done.

Serve over traditional polenta, soft or grilled.

HOLIDAY QUAIL WITH ORANGE GLAZE

SERVES 4

- *8 semi-boned quail*
- *1¾ cup white wine*
- *8 garlic cloves*
- *½ cup dried mushrooms*
- *½ cup raisins*

- *orange glaze (recipe below)*
- *½ Asian pear*
- *¼ bunch flat-leaf parsley*
- *½ lb. ground pork*
- *olive oil*

- *¼ cup Sensational Seasoning*
- *½ cup breadcrumbs*
- *1 egg*

Marinate quail in 1 cup white wine and 6 cloves of garlic for 45 minutes. Soak mushrooms in 1 cup of water for 30 minutes before using. Squeeze out water and chop coarsely. Soak raisins in ½ cup white wine for 20 minutes or until plump. Chop garlic coarsely. Peel Asian pear and chop into small pieces. Dice parsley. Prepare orange glaze (recipe below) and set aside.

Brown ground pork and remaining garlic in oiled frying pan. Add Asian pear, raisins, mushrooms and parsley. When pork is fully cooked add ¼ cup of white wine to de-glaze pan. Add 2 tblsp. Sensational Seasoning and stir. Transfer into a mixing bowl and fold in bread crumbs. Add egg and mix to the consistency of meatloaf.

Stuff each marinated quail with 3 tblsp. each of mixture. Prop breast up and cross legs over cavity. Do not crowd in dish. Paint with olive oil and 2 tblsp. of Sensational Seasoning.

Pre-heat oven at 400⁰. Bake for approximately 15 minutes or until done. Remove from oven and paint with orange glaze. Return to oven and cook for additional 5 minutes or until done. Glaze quail again and serve. Remaining orange glaze can be served on the side.

ORANGE GLAZE

- *3 minced garlic cloves*
- *2 tblsp. finely chopped onion*
- *1 tblsp. butter*

- *½ cup orange juice*
- *¼ cup Grand Marnier liqueur*

In a small frying pan, sauté garlic and onion in butter. Add orange juice and Grand Marnier, and reduce. Serve when sauce has thickened serve.

MY FATHER, SANTO PISTO, AND AUNT JENNY.

S unday was the day the family spent together. Although this time was meant for relaxing, with such a large family the house was always noisy, and music played a big part in our lives.

My father used to play the mandolin, guitar and accordion, all quite well. He loved to sing old Sicilian folk songs and the rest of the family would often join in. I will always remember our house being filled with sweet sounds of the old country

ITALIAN SPECIALTIES

Pisto's Marinara • Italian Sausage Marinara with Pasta • Traditional Polenta • Polenta Torta • Baby Artichoke Frittata • Gnocchi alla Nona • Baby Artichoke Rissotto • Sal's Pig's Feet with Pasta

PISTO'S MARINARA

MAKES ABOUT 1 QUART

- 8 garlic cloves
- 1 med. yellow onion
- olive oil
- ½ bunch Italian flat-leaf parsley
- ½ bunch fresh basil

- 2 28-oz. cans whole, peeled tomatoes
- ¼ tsp. cracked red pepper
- 2 tsp. sugar
- salt & black pepper

Coarsely chop garlic and onion. Remember, the finer the chop the more powerful the flavor. In a large skillet, lightly brown garlic and onion in olive oil. Remove stems from parsley and basil and chop coarsely. Add to skillet. Squeeze in tomatoes with juice. Add red pepper. Add sugar to balance tomato acid. Salt and pepper to taste. Bring to boil, then reduce heat to medium and simmer until sauce thickens, approximately 20-30 minutes.

ITALIAN SAUSAGE MARINARA WITH PASTA

MAKES ABOUT 1 QUART

- 8 garlic cloves
- 1 med. yellow onion
- olive oil
- 2 lbs. Italian sausage
- ½ bunch Italian flat-leaf parsley
- ½ bunch fresh basil

- 2 28-oz. cans whole, peeled Italian tomatoes
- ¼ tsp. ground red pepper
- 2 tsp. sugar
- 1 lb. linguini pasta
- ¼ lb. Romano or Parmesan cheese
- salt & black pepper

Coarsely chop garlic and onion. In a large skillet, lightly brown garlic and onion in olive oil. Add sausage and cook thoroughly. Remove stems from parsley and basil and chop coarsely. Add to skillet. Squeeze in tomatoes with juice. Add red pepper. Stir in sugar to balance tomato acid. Salt and pepper to taste. Bring to boil then reduce to medium heat and simmer until sauce thickens, for approximately 20-30 minutes.

Prepare pasta in rapidly boiling water. Drain and place on serving platter. Pour sauce over pasta. Grate cheese over the dish and serve.

Traditional Polenta

SERVES 4-6

- *2 cups ground corn meal*
- *salt*
- *¼ tsp. each crushed red & black pepper*
- *½ cup butter*
- *1½ cups Reggiano cheese*

Bring 8 cups of salted (using only 1 tblsp.) water to a rapid boil. Pour corn meal into boiling water and stir with a whisk over high heat. Add red and black pepper, butter, salt to taste and cheese and mix thoroughly. After corn meal is mixed, reduce to a medium flame. Stir continuously for 45 minutes.

Remove from heat and serve warm, or pour into a large sheet pan, spreading evenly to cool. The mixture will harden in approximately 20 minutes. Cut into serving size squares. Pre-heat large grill until smoking. Brush polenta with olive oil. Brown on both sides and serve with the sauce of your choice.

Polenta Torta

SERVES 4-6

- *1 cup grated Reggiano cheese*
- *2 tblsp. butter*

Note: make polenta first and cool on baking sheet. Then prepare either the traditional or sausage marinara.

Slice cold polenta with a thread or wire into ⅛-inch slices. On baking sheet alternate polenta with grated cheese and sauce, ending with cheese and a bit of butter. Bake in oven at 400° for approximately 1 hour or until done. Serve hot.

BABY ARTICHOKE FRITTATA

SERVES 4

- *24 baby artichokes*
- *1 med. yellow onion*
- *6 garlic cloves*
- *½ bunch Italian flat-leaf parsley*
- *12 asparagus spears*
- *olive oil*
- *5 tblsp. butter*
- *8 lg. eggs*
- *½ cup bread crumbs*
- *½ cup Reggiano cheese*
- *salt & black pepper*

Clean and prepare baby artichokes. Cook in rapidly boiling water for 3-5 minutes. Drain and let cool. Cut into quarters.

Chop onion, garlic and parsley coarsely. Blanch asparagus in boiling water for 2-3 minutes and cut into ½-inch pieces.

Pour olive oil into pre-heated, non-stick skillet over medium heat. Add 3 tblsp. butter. Sauté onion in skillet until soft. Remove skillet from heat.

In a large bowl, beat eggs until thoroughly mixed. Add garlic, parsley, asparagus, artichokes, bread crumbs, cheese, salt and pepper and mix well. Pour mixture into skillet with onions and let mixture brown slightly, lifting sides occasionally with a spatula.

Preheat oven to 350⁰. Place skillet in oven and bake for 15-20 minutes.

Remove from oven and let cool for 15 minutes. Place a plate over skillet and flip frittata onto plate. Melt butter over the top, sprinkle with a bit of cheese and serve.

MY GRANDFATHER, ALFONSO PISTO, IN SICILY.

Upon arriving in America, my grandfather landed a job with the railroad. This career kept him in New York for the better part of his life. Although he was a good family man, he worked long shifts and odd hours. His wife, Josephine, could not adjust to life in America and Alfonso's new career. She desperately wanted to go home to the peaceful countryside of Sicily. After many months of urging her to stay, he finally agreed to send her home to live with their youngest daughter, Bettina. I still say, if he had brought her to Monterey, she would be here today.

Gnocchi alla Nona

SERVES 6

- *4 lbs. of potatoes*
- *4 cups flour*
- *½ cup melted butter*
- *½ lb. Reggiano cheese*
- *salt*

Boil whole potatoes until soft. Drain, peel and mash. Quickly add flour , butter and sprinkle with salt. Work ingredients into a dough. Break off pieces and shape into sausage-like rolls, about 1-inch thick.

Press each piece with your thumb against the concave surface of a cheese grater or fork to create a ridged pattern. Place gnocchi on floured surface to prevent them from sticking together.

Bring a large pan of salted water to a boil and drop in gnocchi. Remove them with a perforated spoon as soon as they float to the top (after approximately 3 minutes). Cook in small batches to avoid sticking together. Place gnocchi in serving dish, top with marinara sauce and grated cheese.

Baby Artichoke Rissotto

SERVES 4

- *24 baby artichokes*
- *1 lg. yellow onion*
- *4 garlic cloves*
- *¼ lb. prosciutto*
- *1 lb. Italian short grain rice*
- *olive oil*
- *3 tblsp. butter*
- *½ cup white wine*
- *pinch of saffron*
- *6 to 8 cups beef broth*
- *¼ cup heavy cream*
- *½ cup Reggiano cheese*
- *salt & black pepper*

Clean artichokes and remove dark green, outer leaves. Cook in rapidly boiling water for 5-10 minutes or until they can be peirced with a fork. Chop onions and garlic coarsely. Chop prosciutto into small cubes.

Pour olive oil into pre-heated large skillet. Add butter. When butter has melted add onions and garlic. Sauté until soft. Add rice to skillet and stir until slightly brown. Add white wine and stir until wine reduces. Salt and pepper to taste. Begin to add broth, one cup at a time, reducing it before you add the next cup. Add saffron and stir continuously. Fold in artichokes, prosciutto and cream. Preparation time will be approximately 45-60 minutes. Top with cheese and freshly cracked black pepper and serve.

MY GRANDMOTHER, JOSEPHINE PISTO, IN HER SUNDAY BEST.

I inherited my grandmother's love of cooking. Although I didn't know her well, I remember our visits to her home and the joy she brought to our family. It was the time we spent in her family kitchen that perked my interest in traditional Italian cooking. I will always remember her bent over her wood-burning stove, making her incredibly delicious rissotto.

SAL'S PIG'S FEET WITH PASTA

SERVES 6

- *4 pig's feet (cut in halves)*
- *2 cups red wine*
- *10 large garlic cloves*
- *2 bay leaves*
- *olive oil*
- *¼ bunch Italian flat-leaf parsley*
- *salt & black pepper to taste*

- *1 med. yellow onion*
- *2 28-oz. cans chopped tomatoes*
- *¼ tsp. crushed red pepper*
- *1 tsp. sugar*
- *1 lb. linguini pasta*
- *grated Reggiano cheese*

Marinate pig's feet in 1½ cups red wine, 5 garlic cloves and bay leaves. Refrigerate overnight.

Bring a 2-gallon pot of salted water to a rapid boil. Add pig's feet and boil for 1 hour and 45 minutes or until tender. Dry feet thoroughly to prevent splattering when browning.

Coarsely chop garlic, parsley and onion.

Pour olive oil into a large pot. Place over medium heat. When the pan is hot, add pig's feet, salt and pepper, then lightly brown on all sides. Remove feet from pan and add remaining garlic, parsley and onion. Sauté for 2-3 minutes.

De-glaze pan with remaining red wine. Stir over high heat. Add chopped tomatoes and crushed red pepper. Stir in sugar to balance tomato acid. Return feet to pot and cover. Simmer for 1 hour or until tender.

While the meat is simmering, prepare linguini in rapidly boiling water. Drain and place on serving platter. Place pig's feet over pasta, pour sauce over feet, sprinkle with grated cheese and serve.

MY FATHER AND I STROLLING DOWN THE STREETS OF MONTEREY, CIRCA 1945.

As I look back at my childhood, it is the Sunday walks with my father that I cherish most fondly. I found great love and respect for Monterey on these neighborly strolls: the natural beauty, the friendly townspeople, the smell of barbequed fish in the air, and the stories my father told of our history, and his dreams for the future.

GIA PISTO, MY LITTLE PRINCESS.

Like father-like daughter, Gia Pisto spends a great deal of time in the kitchen. I believe children should learn to appreciate a good homecooked meal, and what better way to instill a love for good, healthy food than to put them in the kitchen. Gia loves to cook and she feels she is contributing to our family in the process.

ANTIPASTO

Blackened Scallop Salad • Blackened Rock Fish Salad •
Steamed Artichokes with Garlic Mayonnaise • Stuffed
Artichokes • Stand-up Artichoke Salad • Baby Artichoke with
Pear & Prosciutto • Roasted Garlic • Roasted Bell Peppers •
Grilled Eggplant • Prickly Pear Cactus Salad • Bruschetta •
Old Fashioned Tomato Salad • Classic Caesar Salad

BLACKENED SCALLOP SALAD

SERVES 2

- *4 lg. scallops*
- *1 head Napa cabbage (sliced thin)*
- *4 garlic cloves*
- *olive oil*

- *1 tsp. Sensational Seasoning*
- *½ cup white wine*
- *2 tblsp. balsamic vinegar*
- *1 tblsp. butter*

- *1 lg. orange*
- *salt & black pepper to taste*

Place rinsed cabbage in a 1-gallon pot of boiling water for 2 minutes. Remove from pot and rinse under cold water to retain color.

Pre-heat a large skillet. Chop garlic coarsely. Cover the bottom of skillet with olive oil. Add garlic and salt. Chop cabbage coarsely. Sauté cabbage in skillet for about 1½ minutes.

Rinse and dry scallops. Sprinkle with Sensational Seasoning and salt and pepper to taste. Place in a large pre-heated frying pan, well oiled). Sear on both sides (approximately 1 minute) to lock in juices. De-glaze pan with white wine and balsamic vinegar. Reduce liquid and add a tablespoon of butter.

Cut orange into rings. Arrange cabbage on serving platter. Place orange slices on cabbage. Place scallops on orange slices. Pour sauce over scallops and serve hot.

BLACKENED ROCK FISH SALAD

SERVES 4

- *4 lg. boned rock fish*
- *1 goose neck zucchini*
- *1 green bell pepper*
- *1 red bell pepper*
- *6 asparagus spears*

- *4 green onions*
- *olive oil*
- *2 tsp. Sensational Seasoning*
- *4 tsp. soy sauce*

- *1 tsp. rice vinegar*
- *1 tsp. honey*
- *1 tsp. sesame seeds*
- *1 lb. baby greens*

Cut bell peppers and zucchini into 1-inch thick strips length-wise. Remove root end of green onions. Freshly cut asparagus ends. Paint vegetables with olive oil.

Pre-heat stovetop grill until smoking. Grill vegetables, turning continuously for approximately 6 minutes. Remove from grill. Paint fillets with olive oil on both sides and coat with Sensational Seasoning. Grill fillets for 3 minutes on each side.

Mix soy sauce, vinegar, honey and sesame seeds in a large mixing bowl. Add baby greens and mix well. Place greens on serving platter. Lay fillets over greens and arrange vegetables around the fish and serve.

THE BEGINNINGS OF MY CAREER IN THE RESTAURANT BUSINESS.

I never grew tired of the activity on Fisherman's Wharf. Even when I was helping my father press slacks at the tailor shop, I always found time to meet with my old fishing buddies.

After high school, I attended Monterey Peninsula College by day and worked on the wharf by night. I was the sole employee of a tacky little restaurant, serving as the head fry cook and dishwasher. The owner (I won't mention any names) had some unique techniques for saving a few bucks. He called them his "trade secrets." I can joke about it now only because he has long been out of business and I haven't heard of any harm coming from them. My favorite secret was the preparation of grilled New York steak. Although this item was on the menu, we only had the standard fryer and flat grill, so just before they would leave the kitchen, the owner would brand the steaks with a hot coat hanger. Even with my limited experience in the kitchen, I knew something just wasn't right. It was these experiences that led me to the School of Culinary Arts.

My father knew of my love for the wharf and his pride in my schooling encouraged him to make me a proposition. It was during the mid-1960s when a little soap shop went up for sale on the wharf. My father offered to become my partner in the restaurant business, if I was willing to run it. This was a dream come true and naturally I accepted. We named it "The Captain's Gig" (for it was just about that big). I decorated it in the motif of the era: rock 'n roll posters, bentwood chairs and brass lanterns.

There were just four items on the menu. One of them, fish & chips, caught on like wildfire. Soon my little hole-in-the-wall was serving celebrities like Clint Eastwood and Richard Boone, and it was in this very establishment that I met my future wife, Cheryl. This educational and fun-filled experience whet my appetite for the restaurant business, and I was ready to move on to bigger and better things.

STEAMED ARTICHOKES WITH GARLIC MAYONNAISE

SERVES 4

- *4 lg. artichokes*
- *½ lemon (juice only)*
- *1 bay leaf*
- *2 garlic cloves*

Cut artichokes ½-inch from top cone and clip leaf tips. Squeeze the juice from lemon over artichokes. Steam in 1 inch of boiling water, with bay leaf and garlic cloves, for 30 minutes. Remove and drain by holding artichoke upside down and squeezing. Place on serving dish and fan leaves out around the plate. Serve hot or cold.

PISTO'S GARLIC MAYONNAISE

MAKES 1 CUP+

- *2 eggs*
- *1 tsp. lemon juice*
- *1 tsp. red wine vinegar*
- *½ cup light olive oil*
- *½ tsp. dried mustard*
- *2 garlic cloves*
- *½ tsp. tomato paste*
- *pinch of saffron*
- *salt & black pepper to taste*

Place eggs, salt and pepper, lemon juice, vinegar and dried mustard in a food processor. Process for 8 seconds. With machine running, slowly drizzle oil into mixture. Press garlic. Add garlic, tomato paste and saffron to mixture. Blend until thick. Chill for 1 hour. Spoon mayonnaise into center of each artichoke.

THE WHALING STATION INN RESTAURANT, JUST ABOVE CANNERY ROW AT 763 WAVE ST. IN MONTEREY, CALIFORNIA.

After a few years at the "Gig," I wanted a dinner house, someplace big enough to show Monterey what I could do. I began searching for a location and ran into a few snags. Maybe it was the length of my hair, the flared bell-bottom pants, or the fact that I was Italian. For whatever reason, I couldn't find anyone to rent to me. After months of looking, some friends told me about an old Chinese junk store and boarding house, once called Mow Wo's. Located just above Cannery Row, it was owned by a couple of Italian boys, my old friends Bert Cutino and Ted Balestreri.

Why they hadn't had it condemned, I'll never know. Yet, being a man of vision, I decided to take the chance. My wife, Cheryl, her brothers, Allen, Gip, Kent and Todd, and I, gutted the building and furnished it to resemble one of those New York men's clubs. I named it the Whaling Station Inn Restaurant in memory of those who used to board there. That was over twenty-five years ago and although the place hasn't changed much, it's still going strong, even winning many local, regional and national awards. When people tire of those trendy, all atmosphere no-culinary-talent eateries, they always come back to the Whaling Station.

STUFFED ARTICHOKES

SERVES 4

- *4 lg. artichokes*
- *1 cup seasoned bread crumbs*
- *¼ cup raisins*
- *¼ bunch Italian flat-leaf parsley*
- *3 tsp. olive oil*

Mix bread crumbs with raisins and coarsely chopped parsley. Mix in olive oil as a binding agent. Remove ½-inch of top cone from artichoke and clip leaves. Gently spread leaves to allow for stuffing. Stuff bread crumb mixture between leaves and steam in covered pan with 1-inch of rapidly boiling water for 20-30 minutes, adding more water as needed. Test with a fork to the heart. Place artichokes in a broiler for 3-5 minutes to brown stuffing. Serve warm or at room temperature.

STAND-UP ARTICHOKE SALAD

SERVES 4

- *4 lg. artichokes*
- *1 whole ripe tomato*
- *4 garlic cloves*
- *¼ bunch Italian flat-leaf parsley*
- *½ lemon (juice only)*
- *⅓ cup red wine vinegar*
- *1 tblsp. hot mustard*
- *1 tsp. sugar*
- *¼ cup olive oil*
- *1 lb. baby greens*
- *Calamata olives*
- *salt & black pepper to taste*

Cut ¼-inch off stem. Remove bottom outer leaves by pulling down while your thumb presses against the base of each leaf, leaving a crescent shape. Continue this process until the remaining leaves are a soft yellow. Cut off the top of the cone and scrape out the center to the heart. With a knife, shave the first layer from the stem and crescents, leaving a soft greenish-yellow color. Place artichokes in 2 inches of rapidly boiling salted water for 30-40 minutes, depending on the size of the artichokes. Test for tenderness with a fork to the heart.

While the artichokes are cooking, prepare vinaigrette. Blanch tomato in boiling water for 2-3 minutes. Remove from water and peel. Discard seeds and juice then chop meat into small pieces.

Press garlic and place in mixing bowl. Chop parsley coarsely. Add the juice from lemon, mustard, vinegar, tomato, sugar, parsley, salt and pepper and slowly stir in olive oil. Mix baby greens with vinaigrette. Place greens on serving plates. Dip artichokes in remaining vinaigrette and place them in center of each plate. Garnish with olives and serve.

BABY ARTICHOKE WITH PEAR & PROSCIUTTO

SERVES 2-4

- *12 baby artichokes*
- *1 ripe tomato*
- *4 garlic cloves*
- *¼ bunch Italian flat-leaf parsley*
- *½ lemon (juice only)*
- *1 tblsp. hot mustard*
- *⅓ cup red wine vinegar*
- *1 tsp. sugar*
- *5 tblsp. olive oil*
- *1 lb. baby greens*
- *1 lg. ripe pear*
- *6 thin slices of prosciutto*
- *4 thin slices of Reggiano cheese*
- *salt & freshly ground black pepper to taste*

Clean and prepare baby artichokes. Remove outer leaves until the artichoke is soft and yellow. Cut off ½-inch from top cone. Cook in rapidly boiling water for 2-4 minutes, or until they can be pierced with a fork. Remove from boiling water and rinse with cold water. Cut the chokes in half.

Blanch whole tomatoes in boiling water for 2-3 minutes. Remove from water and peel. Discard seeds and juice, then chop meat into small pieces.

Press garlic cloves and place in mixing bowl. Chop parsley coarsely. Add lemon juice, 4 tblsp. olive oil, mustard, vinegar, tomato, parsley, sugar and salt and pepper to taste. Mix thoroughly.

Mix baby greens with vinaigrette. Remove greens and place on serving plate. Place artichokes on bed of greens. Spoon remaining vinaigrette over artichokes.

Peel pear and cut into thin slices. Arrange pear next to baby greens. Layer prosciutto and cheese over pear slices. Drizzle remaining olive oil over prosciutto, sprinkle with fresh ground black pepper and serve.

ROASTED GARLIC

SERVES 4

- *4 extra-large heads of garlic*
- *extra virgin olive oil*
- *whole oregano*
- *crushed red pepper*
- *salt & black pepper to taste*

Pre-heat oven to 300⁰.

Cut off top of whole garlic heads to expose cloves. Brush with olive oil. Sprinkle with salt, black pepper, red pepper and whole oregano.

Place garlic on baking sheet with a small amount of water. Bake for 1 hour or until the cloves are slightly brown and soft.

Remove from oven and let cool for 5 minutes before serving.

ROASTED BELL PEPPERS

SERVES 4

- *2 red bell peppers*
- *2 yellow bell peppers*
- *2 green bell peppers*
- *3 lg. garlic cloves*
- *2 tsp. dry oregano*
- *¼ bunch fresh basil*
- *¼ cup olive oil*
- *salt & black pepper to taste*

Sear bell peppers over an open flame, turning continuously until the skin begins to blister evenly (you may use a barbecue or a gas stove). Remove peppers from flame and place in a large, covered pot for approximately 30-45 minutes. This process will make the skins easy to remove.

Remove the skins with a knife. Remove and discard stems. Cut open and scrape out the seeds and discard. Cut peppers into ½-inch strips and place in a serving bowl.

Slice garlic cloves into thin slivers and sprinkle over bell peppers. Coarsely chop basil. Sprinkle oregano and basil over bell peppers. Drizzle olive oil over entire dish and serve.

This dish will improve when served the next day. Keep refrigerated.

FISHING BOAT AT SUNRISE ON MONTEREY BAY.

After ten years on Cannery Row, I had the urge to open another restaurant. In 1981 I headed back towards my old stomping grounds—Monterey's Fisherman's Wharf. There, I introduced Domenico's on the Wharf, named after my youngest daughter, Gia Domenica Pisto. This restaurant features the harvests of the sea complemented by locally grown produce, served with a traditional Italian flair. After more thantwo decades of serving California Italian cuisine, I have to say this combination has been quite successful.

In 1991 I had the opportunity to purchase Abalonetti Restaurant, directly across the walk from Domenico's on the Wharf. Owned by the Favalora family, this restaurant had been around for as long as I could remember. Abalonetti specialized in calamari and the menu featured almost a dozen variations. I had always respected the family and their restaurant trademark. Although I enlivened the atmosphere with some serious remodeling, you will still find the restaurant's signature calamari dishes, including the famous Marty 's Special, on the menu. The new Abalonetti Seafood Trattoria, with its fun and casual atmosphere, has become a hit with locals and visitors, as well as with the occasional rock 'n roll star.

Today I am negotiating for the fourth Pisto restaurant. I've already set the menu in my head.

I am most grateful to live and work on the Monterey Peninsula, for it is truly a chef's paradise. Here I can walk out into the fields and pick my own artichokes, hunt for wild mushrooms in the woods and choose my fresh fish right off the boat. I encourage you to experience Monterey County, its heritage and natural beauty as well as its bounty of delectable foods, wines and restaurants.

Grilled Eggplant

SERVES 4-6

- 1 lg. eggplant
- olive oil
- salt & black pepper to taste
- ¼ bunch fresh mint
- 2 lg. garlic cloves
- 2 tblsp. balsamic vinegar

You may choose to barbecue your eggplant or to use a stovetop grill. Grill must be pre-heated until smoking.

Cut eggplant into ½-inch slices. Brush slices with olive oil on both sides. Sprinkle with salt and pepper. Grill eggplant for 5-8 minutes on each side.

Coarsely chop mint. Finely chop garlic cloves. Place on a large serving platter, slightly overlapping each slice with another. Sprinkle with balsamic vinegar, mint and garlic. Drizzle with olive oil. Let sit for 5 minutes to absorb flavors, then serve.

Prickly Pear Cactus Salad

SERVES 2-4

- 2 young cactus leaves
- 1 lg. ripe tomato
- ½ med. white onion
- ½ bunch fresh cilantro
- 2 garlic cloves
- 2 tblsp. olive oil
- 1 shot rum
- ¼ tsp. crushed red pepper
- ½ lemon (juice only)
- salt & black pepper to taste

Wash cactus and remove thorns with a potato peeler. Place in large pot of salted, boiling water. Boil for 3-5 minutes over high heat. Remove from pot and run under cold water. Slice cactus into bite-sized pieces.

Slice tomato and discard seeds and meat, leaving outer shell. Chop tomato, onions garlic and cilantro coarsely.

Pre-heat skillet over high heat. Add olive oil, onions, garlic, and sauté for 5 minutes. Add tomatoes, cactus, cilantro, rum, red pepper, salt and black pepper and lemon juice. Sauté for 3-5 minutes and serve hot.

BRUSCHETTA

SERVES 6-8

- *1 loaf of day-old Italian bread*
- *4 ripe tomatoes*
- *4 lg. garlic cloves*
- *¼ bunch fresh basil*
- *olive oil*
- *salt & black pepper to taste*

Chop ripe tomatoes into small, ¼-inch pieces with a sharp knife.

Sprinkle with salt and black pepper. Press two garlic cloves into a small mixing bowl. Chop basil leaves coarsely and sprinkle on tomatoes. Pour 1 tsp. olive oil into tomato mixture.

Pre-heat stovetop grill over high heat until smoking. Cut bread into thin slices. Brush bread with olive oil on both sides, then toast bread on both sides.

Remove bread from grill and rub the remaining whole garlic cloves over the toasted bread. Place bread on large serving platter. Spoon tomato mixture over bread and serve.

OLD FASHIONED TOMATO SALAD

SERVES 2

- *4 lg. ripe tomatoes*
- *3 lg. garlic cloves*
- *½ lg. red onion*
- *½ bunch fresh basil*
- *6 anchovies*
- *¼ cup olive oil*
- *2 tsp. dry oregano*
- *1 cup pitted Calamata olives*
- *salt & black pepper to taste*

Slice tomatoes into 8 wedges each and place in mixing bowl. Coarsely chop garlic, onion and basil. Chop anchovies into small, bite-sized pieces. Add garlic, onions, basil, anchovies, oregano and olives to mixing bowl. Mix in olive oil and 2 tblsp. water. Season with salt and black pepper to taste. Chill for 1 hour before serving.

CLASSIC CAESAR SALAD

SERVES 4-6

- 6 heads of romaine lettuce
- 1 loaf of day-old Italian bread
- ¾ cup butter
- 6 garlic cloves
- 1½ cups Parmesan cheese
- 2 tsp. fresh-cracked black pepper
- 2 eggs

- 6 anchovies
- 2 tblsp. kosher salt
- ¼ cup red wine vinegar
- 2 lemons (juice only)
- 3 tsp. dry mustard
- 2 tblsp. Worcestershire sauce
- 6 tblsp. extra virgin olive oil

To make croutons, cut bread into bite-sized cubes and place in mixing bowl. Melt butter in small saucepan. Press 4 cloves of garlic into butter, sprinkle with ¼ tsp. of black pepper and stir. Spoon butter mixture over bread. Grate cheese and sprinkle ¼ cup over bread. Pre-heat oven to broil. Place bread on baking sheet. Broil for 2-3 minutes (check frequently so as not to burn), turn and broil for another 2-3 minutes (croutons are done when they are nicely browned). Remove from oven and let cool.

Choose a wooden bowl exclusively for this salad. Rub the bowl with one clove of garlic. The clove will dissolve into the bowl, which will forever retain this flavor.

Remove dark green leaves from lettuce until you reach the heart (leaves are tight and yellow).

Submerge eggs in a pan of boiling water for 1 minute. Remove from pan and set aside in cold water.

Place anchovies in wooden bowl. Add vinegar and crush anchovies into a paste using a wooden spoon. Add kosher salt and continue making paste. Press remaining garlic clove and add to mixture. Add lemon juice, mustard, and Worcestershire sauce and stir. Crack eggs and discard egg whites. Add yoke to mixture and stir. Slowly pour in olive oil, stirring continuously.

Tear lettuce into bite-sized pieces and place in bowl. With tongs, gently mix lettuce with dressing until no residue is found on the bottom of bowl. Mix in croutons and sprinkle with remaining cheese and fresh cracked black pepper.

The Pat Hathaway Collection

THE NATURAL BEAUTY OF THE MONTEREY PENINSULA IS UNMATCHED ANYWHERE IN THE WORLD.   PHOTO BY E.A. COHEN

The Pat Hathaway Collection

THIS RUGGED COASTLINE IS FAMOUS THROUGHOUT THE WORLD AND IS A PERSONAL INSPIRATION FOR ALL OF US WHO LIVE ON THE MONTEREY PENINSULA.

PISTO'S

❖

Sensational Seasoning • Moroccan Seasoning &
Marinade • Imported Italian Olive Oil • Cast Iron
Stovetop Grill • Monterey's Cookin' Video Tapes •
Monterey's Cookin' Newsletter • Domenico's on the
Wharf • The Whaling Station Inn • Abalonetti Seafood
Trattoria • John Pisto's Newest Restaurant

GOURMET PRODUCTS
FROM PISTO'S KITCHEN

Pisto's Select Sensational Seasoning

2.3 OZ. JARS

Pisto's famous Sensational Seasoning serves as an all-purpose gourmet seasoning for seafood dishes, pasta sauces, stews, grilled vegetables, or as a delicious blackening rub on meat, poultry and fish.

$6.95

Pisto's Select Moroccan Seasoning & Marinade

2.35 OZ. JARS

This unusual blend of spices transforms seafood and poultry dishes into exciting entrees with an international flair. Use generously on grilled fish and poultry to create a flavorful crust. Add a few dashes to soups and sauces for an exotic flavor.

$6.95

Pisto's Select Imported Italian Olive Oil

500ML.

Pisto's imported, extra virgin olive oil is cold pressed the old-fashioned way by Italian olive growers in Italy. Selected for its rich, unrefined taste and its compatibility with stove-top cooking.

$14.95

Cast Iron, Stovetop Grill

After months scouring the country for a replacement for his stovetop grill, John found the ideal heavy duty, all purpose, cast iron grill. This grill is versatile and will literally replace your barbecue.

Grill steaks, chicken, fish fillets, prawns, even polenta. It's easy to use and the professional design gives you unequaled capacity, unmatched flavor and a restaurant-quality presentation.

$49.95 each

Monterey's Cookin' Video Tapes

A series of 3 VHS tapes featuring John's favorite recipes recorded from his television show "Monterey's Cookin" are now available.

Tape #1—Sicilian Marinated Crab, Sicilian Crab Pasta, Lazy Man's Cioppino and Pasta with Marinara Sauce

Tape #2—Calamari Cocktail, Calamari St. Tropez, Squid in Ink Sauce, Calamari Stuffing in Vegetable Boats

Tape #3—Brick Chicken, Rack of Lamb, New York Steak, Filet Mignon, Clams & Pasta

$12.95 each

Monterey's Cookin' Newsletter Subscription

Keep up with John's latest recipes, events and products via Monterey's Cookin' newsletter. With your subscription comes a quarterly newsletter filled with recipes from John's cooking show.

The newsletter will be mailed directly to your home and will feature *member's only* special offers on John's products.

$12.95

Ordering Information

Sensational Seasoning, 2.3 oz. jar	$ 6.95
Moroccan Seasoning & Marinade, 2.35 oz. jar	$ 6.95
Pisto's Italian Olive Oil, 500ML (16.9 fl. oz. bottle)	$14.95
Cast Iron Stovetop Grill	$49.95
Monterey's Cookin' VHS tapes	$12.95
Monterey's Cookin' Newsletter Subscription (1 Year)	$12.95
Pisto's "Chef" Gift Pack	$99.95

- All 3 Monterey's Cookin' VHS tapes
- Cast Iron Grill
- 1-Year Subscription to Monterey's Cookin' Newsletter
- Pisto's Italian Olive Oil
- Sensational Seasoning & Moroccan Spice

(All prices subject to change without notice)

To Order:

Prices include shipping within the continental United States.

Send check or money order to:

Pisto's Kitchen

763 Wave Street, Monterey, CA 93940 • (408) 373-3778

DOMENICO'S ON THE WHARF, 50 FISHERMAN'S WHARF, MONTEREY, CALIFORNIA (408) 372-3655.

A local favorite for over a decade, Domenico's on the Wharf offers traditional Italian cuisine, featuring fresh seafood caught each morning and delivered daily to their private loading docks.

From every table you will enjoy spectacular views of Monterey's historic yacht harbor and the never-ending water show provided by playful harbor seals, soaring seagulls, and even an occasional sea otter. The restaurant is known for its formal, yet friendly, ambiance and impeccable service, as well as its one-of-a-kind menu.

Sample from the tantalizing oyster bar and the award-winning wine list while the staff pampers you. One visit to Domenico's on the Wharf and you will become a regular guest too!

THE WHALING STATION INN
RESTAURANT

THE WHALING STATION INN RESTAURANT, 763 WAVE ST., MONTEREY, CALIFORNIA (408) 373-3778.

An extraordinary regional restaurant with an international reputation, the award-winning Whaling Station Inn is known for its continental cuisine, its old world ambiance, and exemplary service.

The Whaling Station offers a full bar, as well as a wonderful selection of wines, including many Monterey and California vintages.

One of the finest old fashioned dinner houses still in existence, the Whaling Station offers both quality and quantity with every meal served.

Offering locally harvested specialties, succulent mesquite grilled steaks, prime rib, house-made pasta and the freshest seafood available, the Whaling Station Inn is a unique Central Coast experience in dining.

Abalonetti
SEAFOOD TRATTORIA
SINCE 1951

ABALONETTI SEAFOOD TRATTORIA, 57 FISHERMAN'S WHARF, MONTEREY, CALIFORNIA (408)373-1851.

Abalonetti Seafood Trattoria offers a new twist to wharfside dining. Its fun and casual atmosphere has been likened to those found in Milan's fashionable dining district. Bright seascape colors greet you as you enter the main dining room, where you are surrounded by views of the bay. Or if you prefer, you may dine outdoors on Abalonetti's private terrace.

The trattoria specializes in Monterey Bay calamari and offers almost a dozen varieties of squid dishes—many found only at Abalonetti Seafood Trattoria!

The tantalizing menu also offers a bountiful antipasto bar, pizza from the wood-burning oven, a fine selection of California wine, and full bar.

Coming Soon . . .

JOHN PISTO, CONTEMPLATING THE FUTURE OF HIS NEWEST RESTAURANT

The latest addition to John's family of restaurants is yet to be named. Slated to open in July of 1994, this restaurant is graced with magnificent picture windows bringing one of the area's finest views of Monterey Bay into your dining experience.

Plans include special beach lighting and an elegant multi-tiered dining area that will provide each guest access to the extraordinary bay view, day or night. Below the main dining room a magnificent wine cellar is being created and will be stocked with one of the area's finest selections of varietals. Although this restaurant will offer a unique atmosphere and menu, John promises to hold true to the Pisto success formula. We can all look forward to another world-class restaurant.

Finiménto

John Pisto, The Man Behind the Apron • Cooking with John Pisto • Thank You! • A Few Definitions • Index • Notes

John Pisto, The Man Behind the Apron

The combination of his Italian heritage, and his sheer determination to perfect recipes made with fresh local ingredients, has earned John Pisto a reputation as an innovator of California Italian restaurants and recipes.

John loves nothing more than cooking and he has cooked for and with many of the world's finest chefs, including Julia Child and world famous French chef Paul Bocuse. In 1991, John was the West Coast guest chef with legendary Paul Prudhomme at the Galerie Blue Dog Cajun Feast in Carmel, California, and in 1992, a celebrity chef at the American School of Cooking in Kansas City, Missouri. He has also shared the stage with celebrity chef Martin Yan at Monterey County's famous Squid Festival.

As a children's advocate, John has created educational programs for elementary school children throughout the Monterey area. He has worked with the Artichoke Advisory Board, as well as the California Seafood Council & the Department of Education on "Food Education" projects to be distributed nation wide.

For the past 2½ years, John has hosted his own television cooking show on MPI Cable Television, Channel 2. The show, "Monterey's Cookin' Pisto Style," features restaurant specialties viewers can cook at home. Due to the favorable response, he has released a series of home videos taken from the show as well as a quarterly newsletter featuring his recipes and cooking techniques. John has also begun distributing his own gourmet products throughout California.

John is the owner of three-award-winning restaurants on the Monterey Peninsula: The Whaling Station Inn Restaurant, Abalonetti Seafood Trattoria, and Domenico's on the Wharf. A fourth, as yet unnamed, restaurant on Cannery Row will open in July of 1994.

COOKING WITH JOHN PISTO

I want to clarify a few issues that came up as I was preparing this book. Most professional chefs, myself included, do not cook from recipes. I'm not saying that I don't look at recipes. In fact, I have hundreds of cookbooks at home. Chefs are always on the lookout for new ideas and different ways of preparing dishes, but you will never find me in the kitchen with a cookbook open, doling out ingredients with a menagerie of measuring cups and teaspoons. I cook by taste, by memory, by touch and, most often, by inspiration.

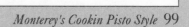

JOHN PISTO AT HOME IN HIS KITCHEN.

I want you to know that I've done my best to translate my pinches, dashes and handfuls into teaspoons, tablespoons and cups, but if you're not satisfied with the way a dish comes out, for heaven's sake experiment and above all taste it . . . taste it as you're cooking it . . . and taste it after you're finished with it. Learning how to identify what you taste is what makes a good cook.

People are always asking me what the secret is to my cooking. I believe the key to fine cooking is to never cook because you have to. You should cook only when there is joy in your heart and you want to share that joy with those at the table.

I'll tell you another secret. I never let my chefs cook when they're in a bad mood. I send them home. However, I almost never have to do this because those who choose this profession choose it because they love to cook. I know that for myself cooking brings me joy, and sharing that joy with those I love is what makes me happiest of all.

I hope you enjoy this humble book and that it encourages you to experiment and experience the lighter, warmer, funnier side of cooking.

I'd love to hear from you and have your comments about the book and my recipes:

Pisto's Kitchen
763 Wave St.
Monterey, CA 93940

THANK YOU!

One of the nice things about writing this book is that it gives me a chance to thank some of the many folks who have meant so much to me over the years.

To my loving wife Cheryl,
who helped make it all possible and worthwhile!

To Dana,
thank you for being more than just a son!

To Gia, my youngest,
in whose heart a great chef resides.

To all of my children,
many of whom have worked in the restaurants, all of whom have brought me great joy!

To my longtime partner and friend, Devin McGilloway, and his lovely wife Jan,
for their contribution to making the restaurants such a success.

To Nate and his wonderful family,
my partner in good food.

To my mentor, Jack Allen, who taught me what really good food was, and who could write a dozen books himself.

To Louie Menedez, another source of great wisdom for me along the way.

To the hundreds of loyal, hardworking employees, past and present, who have worked with me to create the finest restaurants possible.

To Patrick Mercurio,
for our memorable trips to France & Italy together

To Sal Balesteri and his lovely wife Linda ,
for their help, their friendship and their honesty.

To Ted Balestreri and Burt Cutino ,
for being such good friends and such prestigious neighbors.

To Tony and Barbara Ricciardi,
my porcini hunting pals.

To Bill Rice ,
for the good times ahead and behind, for his succinct advice in the preparation of this book, and for his kind words that serve as the forward.

To Mike Goodenough and his beautiful wife Lee,
my friend and co-host on Monterey's Cookin',

To my uncle Tom,
whose influence meant much to me over the years.

To each and every one of my patrons,
who make every day a pleasure.

To the film crew of Monterey Peninsula Cable, who bring their talent and appetites to every shoot.

To Consolidated Factors, Monterey Fish, and Luce-Carmel Meats, for their constant support and supply of the freshest possible products.

To Al Pierleoni,
a good friend with good advice.

To Rebecca & Craig Riddell,
for their tenacity in sticking with me.

To so many others who, although not forgotten, are far to numerous too mention.

JOHN PISTO, HIS WIFE CHERYL AND DAUGHTER GIA.

The Pisto family lives in Monterey, California, near famed Pebble Beach and Carmel-By-The-Sea. For the Pistos the restaurants are a culmination of their own personal goals and successes. Today, John still makes daily trips in search of the finest and freshest ingredients for his restaurants. John is actively involved with each of his restaurants, including menu preparation, planning and staff training. In any given week, John will alternate between his restaurants' kitchens, working with staff and assuring his patrons receive the very finest dining experience.

His wife Cheryl, is involved in both the restaurants and the community.

Gia Pisto, his youngest daughter, is a promising chef herself and regularly contributes to Dad's newsletter.

Dana Pisto is the manager of Abalonetti Seafood Trattoria and expects to operate John's latest restaurant, opening on Cannery Row in early July of 1994.

John's elder daughters work at the Whaling Station Inn and in administration of the restaurants.

A Few Definitions

ABBONDANZA: to have in abundance and in great variety.

BOCCE BALL: an Italian variety of lawn bowling. The object is to come closest to the pin while knocking opponents' balls away.

BLANCH: (to pre-cook) preheating food in either boiling water or steam.

BLACKENING: the process of heavily coating meat or fish with spices, and seasoning, and then grilling or barbecuing to seal the juices in.

BRAISE: to cook food in a small amount of liquid or steam, in a covered container, so that it cooks slowly.

BREADED: to cover food with crumbs of bread or other food.

CANNERIES: the factories used to can sardines and other fish along Monterey's Cannery Row.

CAST IRON GRILL: used for grilling food indoors on top of the stove.

FELUCCAS: a traditional Mediterranean sailboat used for fishing by the Italians who first immigrated to Monterey. At the turn of the century they dotted the bay. A decade later, with the success of the lampara net, they would be replaced by Monterey clippers.

GARNISH: to embellish or decorate the main dish with ingredients that add color or flavor. Traditional garnishes include paprika, lemons, parsley, radish, carrots, olives, etc.

GRILL: to cook food with direct heat. Also an appliance used for cooking.

PARCHMENT PAPER: Heavy paper available in fine butcher chops.

ROAST: to cook uncovered with heated air such as in an oven.

SHELL: to remove the outer shell from crabs, mussels, clams, etc., so as to access the inner meat.

SIMMER: to cook in liquid just below boiling.

SPAGHETTI HILL: the area in Monterey in which the original settlers were predominately Italian.

INDEX OF RECIPES & PHOTOS

A GROUP OF WELL DRESSED ITALIANS HEADING OUT FOR A MEETING ON THE BAY.

NOTES

MONTEREY'S HISTORIC FISHERMAN'S WHARF.

NOTES

CLOSE-UP OF FISHING BOAT

NOTES